enrich-e-matics

3RD EDITION

BOOK 4

Anne Joshua

MA, Dip Ed (Syd); MSc (Oxon)

enrich-e-matics
3ʳᵈ EDITION

Dear Teachers, Students and Parents,

Thank you for purchasing *Enrich-e-matics 3rd Edition*. This is the fourth of a series of six books designed to develop and enrich students' problem-solving skills. *Enrich-e-matics 3rd Edition* deepens students' mathematical concepts and encourages flexibility of thinking along with a willingness to tackle challenging and fascinating problems. The series was originally designed to cater for the mathematically able student but was also found to be a useful tool for all schools wishing to strengthen their students' mathematical understanding.

What is different about *Enrich-e-matics 3rd Edition*?

Enrich-e-matics 3rd Edition is much more than a collection of puzzles and difficult problems. The exercises are *graded*. Concepts and strategies are developed throughout the series to provide for a systematic development of problem-solving and mathematical ability.

The exercises and activities have been grouped into mathematics strands—**Number, Patterns & Algebra, Chance & Data, Measurement, Space** and **Working Mathematically**— with hundreds of new problems added. This allows students and teachers to work systematically through a number of similar problems focusing on one area of mathematics. It also allows flexibility of programming so that material from different strands can be integrated. The strand is indicated on each page by an icon. Themes are introduced and developed throughout the series. The answers for all problems are included in a removable section at the back of the book.

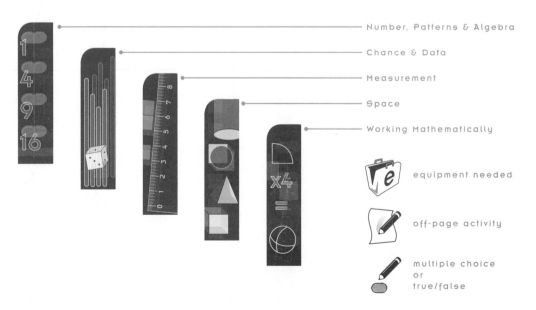

Number, Patterns & Algebra

Chance & Data

Measurement

Space

Working Mathematically

equipment needed

off-page activity

multiple choice
or
true/false

In *Enrich-e-matics 3rd Edition* explanations and worked examples are highlighted. The space for students to write answers and show their working has been maximised in this new edition. An icon has been used to show where students may need extra paper or equipment to complete the problems. Multiple choice and true/false questions use shaded bubbles similar to those used in state and national test papers.

Enrich-e-matics 3rd Edition is designed to meet the needs of students by:

- providing challenging problems for enrichment and extension
- reinforcing concepts and skills
- developing problem-solving strategies and extending mathematical insight, ability and logical thought
- providing opportunities to experience the joy of problem solving
- providing a ready source of challenging problems to prepare students for mathematics competitions

all of which build the foundation for excellence in mathematics.

The *Enrich-e-matics* series may be used to supplement and be integrated into the school's mathematics program.

The *Enrich-e-matics 3rd Edition Teacher's Book* is available to assist teachers implement the enrichment program in their school. It is a most valuable resource containing teaching suggestions, worked solutions and reproducible material. Most importantly it also contains highly valued screening tests that help to identify mathematical ability.

Who can use this book?

Enrich-e-matics 3rd Edition Book 4 may be used by:

- a group of able students working together in class
- classes in selective schools or maths extension groups
- an individual student at home.

The books have been extensively trialled, over several years, with students aged 6 to 15 in schools and at various camps for gifted and talented students. *Enrich-e-matics 3rd Edition Book 4* is aimed at 9 to 11 year olds.

To gain the maximum advantage from the series encourage students to discuss their solutions in small groups, with their teacher or with parents at home. This discussion of ideas enhances learning.

I hope that you will find *Enrich-e-matics 3rd Edition* enjoyable and challenging, and that you remain curious and motivated mathematics students.

Anne Joshua

Contents

ANSWERS
lift-out at the back of book

Patterns and sequences

Each group of numbers follows a pattern. Find the patterns by writing down differences between pairs of numbers. For each one write down the next three numbers.

1 5, 9, 13, 17, _____, _____, _____

2 23, 30, 37, 44, _____, _____, _____

3 4, 9, 14, 19, _____, _____, _____

4 27, 23, 19, 15, _____, _____, _____

5 61, 55, 49, 43, _____, _____, _____

6 100, 97, 94, 91, _____, _____, _____

7 4, 8, 12, 16, _____, _____, _____

8 1, 7, 13, 19, _____, _____, _____

9 12, 23, 34, 45, _____, _____, _____

10 22, 33, 44, 55, _____, _____, _____

11 1, $1\frac{1}{2}$, 2, $2\frac{1}{2}$, _____, _____, _____

12 6, $5\frac{1}{2}$, 5, $4\frac{1}{2}$, _____, _____, _____

13 1, 2, 5, 6, 9, 10, _____, _____, _____

14 1, 2, 4, 5, 7, 8, _____, _____, _____

15 1, 3, 10, 12, 19, 21, _____, _____, _____

16 58, 56, 55, 53, 52, 50, _____, _____, _____

17 47, 43, 41, 37, 35, 31, _____, _____, _____

18 65, 58, 54, 47, 43, 36, _____, _____, _____

Find my rule

In each exercise, find the rule connecting the numbers in the first row with those in the second row. What is the missing number? Put it in the empty box.

1

					RULE
3	7	4	8	2	
6	10	7	11		

2

					RULE
7	12	8	9	15	
3	8	4	5		

3

4	2	7	5	3	
8	4	14	10		

4

6	1	8	10	4	
13	3	17	21		

5

1	2	3	4	5	
9	8	7	6		

6

3	4	5	6	7	
17	16	15	14		

7

9	7	12	6	10	
15	13	18	12		

8

6	3	9	11	4	
16	13	19	21		

9

6	3	9	7	2	
60	30	90	70		

10

1	3	5	7	9	
3	7	11	15		

11

6	3	7	8	2	
11	5	13	15		

12

1	2	3	4	5	
9	19	29	39		

13

6	9	3	7	5	
61	91	31	71		

14

6	9	13	17	5	
1	4	8	12		

15

14	8	10	18	6	
7	4	5	9		

16

3	6	4	7	1	
15	30	20	35		

17

3	6	4	7	1	
14	17	15	18		

18

23	16	14	17	21	
10	3	1	4		

Missing numbers

In each exercise, find the rule connecting the numbers in the first row with those in the second row. What is the missing number? Put it in the empty box.

1   RULE

4	7	3	8	2	
24	42	18	48		

2   RULE

44	12	45	20	13	
36	4	37	12		

3

5	1	3	4	7	
20	4	12	16		

4

5	2	1	3	6	
55	22	11	33		

5

4	7	3	8	9	
8	14	6	16		

6

4	7	3	8	9	
7	13	5	15		

7

4	7	3	8	9	
9	15	7	17		

8

7	3	5	2	6	
69	29	49	19		

9

8	4	3	7	1	
84	44	34	74		

10

8	4	14	18	20	
3	1	6	8		

11

8	1	3	7	5	
18	4	8	16		

12

8	1	3	7	5	
24	3	9	21		

13

8	1	3	7	5	
23	2	8	20		

14

2	4	1	7	8	
7	13	4	22		

15

5	7	4	8	12	
25	35	20	40		

16

5	7	4	8	12	
24	34	19	39		

17

5	7	4	8	1	
17	23	14	26		

18

5	7	4	8	2	
8	12	6	14		

19

5	7	4	3	1	
25	49	16	9		

20

6	2	3	8	1	
35	3	8	63		

Find two numbers

I am thinking of two numbers. What are my two numbers if:

	their **sum** is:	and their **product** is	My two numbers
1	5	4	_____ _____
2	5	6	_____ _____
3	7	10	_____ _____
4	7	6	_____ _____
5	7	12	_____ _____
6	8	7	_____ _____
7	8	15	_____ _____
8	8	12	_____ _____
9	10	25	_____ _____
10	10	16	_____ _____
11	10	24	_____ _____
12	11	18	_____ _____
13	11	30	_____ _____
14	11	28	_____ _____
15	11	10	_____ _____
16	12	36	_____ _____
17	12	11	_____ _____
18	12	35	_____ _____
19	12	32	_____ _____
20	12	27	_____ _____

	their **sum** is:	and their **difference** is	My two numbers
21	11	1	_____ _____
22	11	5	_____ _____
23	13	11	_____ _____
24	13	1	_____ _____
25	13	7	_____ _____
26	18	2	_____ _____
27	18	4	_____ _____
28	18	16	_____ _____
29	20	18	_____ _____
30	20	10	_____ _____

Exploring numbers

The numbers 5, 8 and 9 are one-digit numbers.

The numbers 23, 47 and 88 are two-digit numbers.

The numbers 347, 101 and 928 are three-digit numbers.

1 What is the largest two-digit number? _____

2 What is the smallest two-digit number? _____

3 What is the largest three-digit number? _____

4 What is the smallest three-digit number? _____

5 What is the largest two-digit number in which no numeral is repeated? _____

6 Write down the smallest three-digit number
that uses the numerals 1 and 3 only once. _____

7 What is the largest three-digit number in which no numeral is repeated? _____

8 What is the smallest three-digit number that uses the numeral 0 once? _____

9 Write down the smallest three-digit
number that uses three different numerals. _____

10 What is the largest three-digit number that uses two different numerals? _____

11 What is the smallest three-digit number that uses the numeral 9? _____

12 What is the largest three-digit number that uses the numerals 2 and 7? _____

13 How many one-digit counting numbers are there? _____

14 How many two-digit counting numbers are there? _____

15 How many two-digit numbers use the numeral 5? _____

16 How many two-digit numbers do not use the numeral 5? _____

17 Write down the smallest three-digit odd number. _____

18 Write down the largest three-digit number divisible by 5. _____

19 Write down the smallest three-digit number divisible by 4. _____

20 Write down the largest three-digit number divisible by 3. _____

Shape values

In every large square, each symbol has a different value. The sum of each row and column is given, and from them you can work out the values of the symbols.

For example, in the first row of square 1 you can see that ☐ = 5.

When you write the numbers in, you see that in the first column

5 + ☐ + ☐ = 13, so ☐ = 4.

The other symbols can be found in the same way. **1**

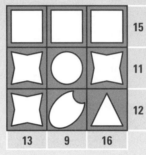

This is how you begin.

2

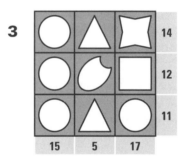

3

4

5

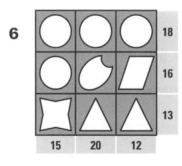

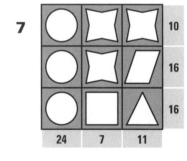

6

7

8

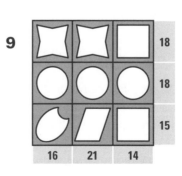

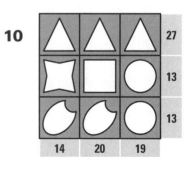

9

10

The four operations

Follow the rules shown in the left-hand columns to complete these tables.
In every case, □ is larger than △.

1

rule												
□	5	8	6							8		
△	2			3	7				3			
□ + △	7	11		9		6	10	11	11			
□ − △	3		4		2	2	4				1	3
□ × △	10						30	18	27	56	42	40

2

rule												
□	4	5	7			5	4					
△	3	2										
△ × △					16	4	4	1	9	4	25	49
□ + △			6	5		8		8				15
□ × △		14	5	6			7			10	30	

3

rule												
□	4	7		8								
△	3	5	1	3		8	2	4				
2 × □			4	10				16			12	20
□ − △				7	2				1	6	3	
□ × △						14	24	32	20	27		30

4

rule												
□	9	10		12	24		24	8			18	
△	3		3			5				2		
3 × △		6						12	27	12		
□ + △		15		27				45	32	20	24	24
□ ÷ △			2		4	4						7

Table squares

You have often been asked to complete addition table squares like the example in exercise 2. The challenge in the other squares is to find the numbers that must be added as well to complete the squares.

In example 1, you are shown which numbers to look for first.

1

+			4	
		7		10
7			11	15
	12		13	
			11	

What number must be added to 7 to make 15 ?

What number must be added to 4 to make 13 ?

2

+	5	3	6	4
2	7	5		
7	12			
1	6			
8				

3

+	4			
7	11	8		
		13	19	
			15	16
				9

4

+		5		
	25	19		
10			18	
		12	15	
	14			9

5

+	2			
	16	8		
	7			13
		20		19
			4	

6

+		3		
			11	
			15	17
	14	5		
	19		14	

7

+	12			
	20			
		15	8	
	17	19		
7			14	10

8

+		10		
		9	14	
	11	15	8	
	13			
		20		

9

+			8	
	13	7		
		10	13	
			16	20
	17			

10

+				9
		13		
			8	11
	8			13
7		12		

8

Letters and symbols

In these equations, each letter or symbol represents a digit. Some of them have the same value. Can you replace them with the correct digits?

For example : $D + D + 3 = 15$ $D = 6$

1 $A \times A = A$ $A = $ _____

2 $B \times B = B + B$ $B = $ _____

3 $C \times C = 16$ $C = $ _____

4 $D \times D \times D = 8$ $D = $ _____

5 $E \times E \times E = 1$ $E = $ _____

6 $P + P + P + P + P = 0$ $P = $ _____

7 $Q + Q + Q + Q = 24$ $Q = $ _____

8 $F \times F \times F = 27$ $F = $ _____

9 $G \times G = 20 + G$ $G = $ _____

10 $M \times M = 30 + M$ $M = $ _____

11 $26 - L = 21$ $L = $ _____

12 $26 - N - N = 20$ $N = $ _____

13 $26 - R - R - R = 14$ $R = $ _____

14 $H + H + H + H + H = 20$ $H = $ _____

15 $J + J + J + J = 20$ $J = $ _____

16 $P + P + P = 10 + P$ $P = $ _____

17 $Y + Y + Y = Z + Z$ $Y = $ _____ $Z = $ _____

18 $W + W + W + W = V + V + V$ $W = $ _____ $V = $ _____

19 $K + K + K = U + U + U + U + U$ $K = $ _____ $U = $ _____

20 $T + 1 = 10$ $T = $ _____

21 $Z \times Z + 1 = 10$ $Z = $ _____

22 $S + S + 2 = 10$ $S = $ _____

23 $X + X - 4 = 10$ $X = $ _____

24 $\heartsuit + 9 = 17$ $\heartsuit = $ _____

25 $\spadesuit \times \spadesuit + 1 = 17$ $\spadesuit = $ _____

What's my message?

In these messages, letters have replaced numbers. Can you work out the problems below each message and so find out what I am saying? (Note that **O** represents the letter O, *not* the number 0.)

1

___ ___ ___ ___   ___   ___ ___ ___ ___   ___ ___ ___ ___ ___ ___ ___
 5   7   6   3   7   9   8   8   1   4   3   3   0   3   2   1

$N \times N = N + N$	$N - N = K$	$E + N = H$
$D + D = N$	$D + K = D$	$A - N = H$
$N + N + N = V$	$N \times N \times N = O$	$H + W = G$
$W \div N = N$	$E \times E = G$	$W + W = O$
$V - N = W$	$E + W = A$	
$E + E = V$	$V + D = A$	

2

___ ___ ___   ___ ___ ___   ___ ___ ___ ___ ___ ___
 9   5   4   3   1   8   7   6   8   2   8   1

$R \times R = R$	$A \times A = Y$
$R + R = V$	$Y - L = A$
$V + V = U$	$U + U = E$
$U + R = O$	$V + C = Y$
$A + V = O$	$A + O = E$
$L - U = V$	$Y - O = U$
$V \times A = L$	$L + O = RR$

Square puzzles

Find the values of the letters **A**, **B**, **C**, **D** and **E** in these squares. The sums of the rows and columns are given, and only the numbers 1, 2, 3, 4 and 5 have been used.

Using the value of the one letter given for each square, work out the values of the other letters and complete the grid.

1

E	C	C	9
E	B	A	9
B	D	A	8
11	7	8	

A	B	C	D	E
				5

5			9
5			9
			8
11	7	8	

2

A	B	C	12
A	C	E	8
D	D	E	5
8	11	6	

A	B	C	D	E
3				

3			12
3			8
			5
8	11	6	

3

B	A	C	8
D	E	E	11
D	A	C	6
11	8	6	

A	B	C	D	E
2				

	2		8
			11
	2		6
11	8	6	

4

A	E	A	13
B	C	D	6
B	E	C	9
6	13	9	

A	B	C	D	E
	1			

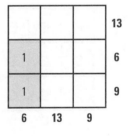

			13
1			6
1			9
6	13	9	

5

D	E	C	8
B	A	C	12
C	A	D	11
10	9	12	

A	B	C	D	E
			2	

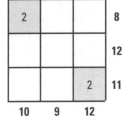

2			8
			12
		2	11
10	9	12	

Find the values

Find the values of the letters **A**, **B**, **C**, **D** and **E** in these squares. The sums of the rows and columns are given, and only the numbers 1, 2, 3, 4 and 5 have been used.

Using the value of the one letter given for each square, work out the values of the other letters and complete the grid. You will have to use trial and error to work out the value of some of the letters!

1

B	B	E
D	C	E
A	D	B

11
11
6

6   9   13

A   B   C   D   E

___   3   ___   ___   ___

3	3	
		3

11
11
6

6   9   13

2

C	B	E
B	D	A
E	E	C

7
9
8

7   8   9

A   B   C   D   E

___ ___ ___ ___ 2

		2
2	2	

7
9
8

7   8   9

3

C	B	D
A	E	C
D	C	B

9
9
9

8   10   9

A   B   C   D   E

___ ___ ___ 4 ___

		4
4		

9
9
9

8   10   9

4

D	E	B
D	C	E
A	B	C

9
8
11

4   12   12

A   B   C   D   E

___ ___ ___ 1 ___

1		
1		

9
8
11

4   12   12

5

D	B	C
B	E	A
A	C	D

11
8
10

12   7   10

A   B   C   D   E

___ ___ 2 ___ ___

		2
	2	

11
8
10

12   7   10

Odd and even

1 Complete these tables.

a

+	2	4	6
2			
4			
6			

even (top), *even* (side)

b

×	2	4	6
2			
4			
6			

even (top), *even* (side)

c

+	1	3	5
1			
3			
5			

odd (top), *odd* (side)

d

×	1	3	5
1			
3			
5			

odd (top), *odd* (side)

e

+	2	4	6
1			
3			
5			

even (top), *odd* (side)

f

×	2	4	6
1			
3			
5			

even (top), *odd* (side)

2 Now use the results you have obtained to complete the next tables, in which O means 'odd' and E means 'even'.

a

+	O	E
O		
E		

b

×	O	E
O		
E		

3 Complete these sentences using the words 'even', 'odd' or 'either even or odd'.

a The sum of two even numbers is always _____

b The sum of three even numbers is always _____

c The sum of four even numbers is always _____

d The product of two even numbers is always _____

e The sum of two odd numbers is always _____

f The sum of three odd numbers is always _____

g The sum of four odd numbers is always _____

h The product of two odd numbers is always _____

i The product of three odd numbers is always _____

j The product of any number of odd numbers is always _____

k The difference between two odd numbers is _____

l The product of an even number and an odd number is _____

m The quotient (result of division) of an even number and an even number is _____

Find three numbers

In each question below, I am thinking of three different numbers: $\square$, $\triangle$ and $\bigcirc$. Using the clues given, can you find them? (Guess and check is a helpful strategy.)

1
$$\triangle + \triangle = 14$$
$$\triangle + \bigcirc = 11$$
$$\square + \bigcirc = 9$$
$$\square + \triangle = \bigcirc + \bigcirc + \bigcirc$$

2
$$\triangle + \triangle + \triangle = 12$$
$$\triangle \times \square = 24$$
$$\bigcirc + \triangle = 12$$
$$\square - \triangle = \bigcirc - \square$$

3
$$\bigcirc + \triangle = 15$$
$$\bigcirc - \triangle = 7$$
$$\triangle + \triangle = \square$$
$$\triangle + \square = 12$$

4
$$\triangle + \triangle + \triangle = \bigcirc$$
$$\triangle + \bigcirc = 12$$
$$\bigcirc - \triangle = 6$$
$$\square + \triangle = 11$$

5
$$\square + \square + \square + \square + \square = \triangle$$
$$\triangle + \square = 12$$
$$\triangle - \square = 8$$
$$\triangle - \bigcirc = 3$$
$$\bigcirc - \square = 5$$

6
$$\square = \triangle + 7$$
$$\square + \triangle = 17$$
$$\bigcirc = \triangle + 2$$
$$\triangle + \bigcirc = \square$$
$$\square + \triangle + \bigcirc = 24$$

7
$$\square + 1 = \triangle$$
$$\triangle + 1 = \bigcirc$$
$$\square + \triangle = 15$$
$$\triangle + \bigcirc = 17$$
$$\bigcirc - \square = 2$$

8
$$\square + \square = \triangle$$
$$\square + \triangle = 9$$
$$\triangle + \triangle = \bigcirc$$
$$\bigcirc - \square = 9$$
$$\triangle \div \square = 2$$

Number sentences

1 Using any combination of the symbols **+**, **−**, **×** and **÷**, and also brackets **( )**, make true sentences for each of the number groups in this exercise.

The order of operations is very important. The numbers in brackets must always be worked first, and you must always multiply and divide before you add or subtract. For example:

$8 - 4 \times 2 \times 1 = 0$ (Find the product of $4 \times 2 \times 1$ first.)

$(8 - 4) \times 2 \times 1 = 8$ (Work out the bracket first.)

$8 + 4 \div 2 - 1 = 9$ (Do $4 \div 2$ first.)

$(8 + 4) \div (2 - 1) = 12$ (Do brackets first.)

$(8 + 4) \div 2 - 1 = 5$ (Do brackets first, so work out $12 \div 2 - 1 = 6 - 1$.)

a   8   4   2   1 = 1   **b**   8   4   2   1 = 2

c   8   4   2   1 = 3   **d**   8   4   2   1 = 4

e   (8   4)   (2   1) = 4   **f**   8   4   2   1 = 5

g   8   4   2   1 = 6   **h**   (8   4)   (2   1) = 6

i   8   4   2   1 = 7   **j**   8   (4   2   1) = 8

k   8   4   2   1 = 9   **l**   8   4   2   1 = 10

m   8   4   2   1 = 11   **n**   (8   4)   (2   1) = 12

o   8   4   2   1 = 13   **p**   8   4   2   1 = 14

q   8   4   2   1 = 15   **r**   8   (4   2)   1 = 15

s   8   (4   2)   1 = 16   **t**   8   4   2   1 = 24

Note that for most of these problems, there is more than one solution.

2 Using four twos, you can write the following number sentences:

$22 \div 2 + 2 = 13$ $2^2 + 2 - 2 = 4$

$2 \times 2 \times 2 \div 2 = 4$ $2 \times 2 + 2 - 2 = 4$

$2 + 2 + 2 - 2 = 4$

Write true sentences for the following numbers, using four 2s and any combination of the symbols +, −, × and ÷.

a   5 _____   **b**   16 _____

c   8 _____   **d**   44 _____

e   26 _____

Magic squares

In a magic square, the numbers of all horizontal, vertical and diagonal lines have the same total—the magic number.

1 In the magic squares below, the numbers from 1 to 16 are each used only once and the magic number is 34. Can you complete the squares?

a

	15		4
12			
8	10		5
13	3		16

b

13		12	1
		6	
2		7	14
	5		

2 Sometimes, when you are asked to complete magic squares, *you* have to find the magic number. In the following examples, look for any vertical, horizontal or diagonal line in which all four numbers are given. The sum of these four is the magic number. Write the magic number below each magic square.

Hint: In square **a**, the magic number is the sum of the numbers in the third column.

a

10		4	
	18	11	6
17	2	9	
	13	16	

b

1	14		12
	4	9	
	5	16	
8			

c

		8	13
16	5	10	7
	6		4
	12	3	

___   ___   ___

Square differences

Remember that to square a number is to multiply it by itself.

$$2^2 = 2 \times 2 \qquad 3^2 = 3 \times 3 \qquad 4^2 = 4 \times 4 \qquad 5^2 = 5 \times 5$$

Continue each of these number patterns for two more lines. Check the patterns by working out each line.

1
$2^2 - 0^2 = 2 \times 2 = 4$
$3^2 - 1^2 = 2 \times 4 = 8$
$4^2 - 2^2 = 2 \times 6 = 12$

_____

_____

2
$3^2 - 0^2 = 3 \times 3 = 9$
$4^2 - 1^2 = 3 \times 5 = 15$
$5^2 - 2^2 = 3 \times 7 = 21$

_____

_____

3
$4^2 - 0^2 = 4 \times 4 = 16$
$5^2 - 1^2 = 4 \times 6 = 24$
$6^2 - 2^2 = 4 \times 8 = 32$

_____

_____

4
$5^2 - 0^2 = 5 \times 5 = 25$
$6^2 - 1^2 = 5 \times 7 = 35$
$7^2 - 2^2 = 5 \times 9 = 45$

_____

_____

5
$3^2 - 1^2 = 2 \times 4 = 4 \times 2 = 8$
$5^2 - 3^2 = 2 \times 8 = 4 \times 4 = 16$
$7^2 - 5^2 = 2 \times 12 = 4 \times 6 = 24$

_____

_____

6
$2^2 - 0^2 = 2 \times 2 = 4 \times 1 = 4$
$4^2 - 2^2 = 2 \times 6 = 4 \times 3 = 12$
$6^2 - 4^2 = 2 \times 10 = 4 \times 5 = 20$

_____

_____

7
$1^2 - 0^2 = 1 + 0 = 1$
$2^2 - 1^2 = 2 + 1 = 3$
$3^2 - 2^2 = 3 + 2 = 5$

_____

_____

8
$2^2 - 1^2 = 1 \times 3 = 3$
$3^2 - 1^2 = 2 \times 4 = 8$
$4^2 - 1^2 = 3 \times 5 = 15$

_____

_____

9
$3^2 - 2^2 = 1 \times 5 = 5$
$4^2 - 2^2 = 2 \times 6 = 12$
$5^2 - 2^2 = 3 \times 7 = 21$

_____

_____

10
$4^2 - 3^2 + 2^2 - 1^2 = 4 + 3 + 2 + 1$
$5^2 - 4^2 + 3^2 - 2^2 = 5 + 4 + 3 + 2$
$6^2 - 5^2 + 4^2 - 3^2 = 6 + 5 + 4 + 3$

_____

_____

Can you make up some number patterns of your own using square differences?

Primes

A prime number is a counting number that has exactly two factors (and no more).

The factors of 5 are 5 and 1.

5 is a prime number.

The factors of 6 are 6, 3, 2 and 1.

6 is not a prime number.

If a number has more than two factors, it is called a composite number: 6 is a composite number.

2 is the only even prime number.

1 is neither a prime nor a composite number.

$$5 = 5 \times 1$$
so 5 is a prime number

$$6 = 2 \times 3$$
so 6 is a composite number

1 a Draw up a table like this for all numbers from 2 to 40.

Number	Factors	Number of factors
2	1, 2	2
3	1, 3	2
4	1, 2, 4	3
5	1, 5	2
6	1, 2, 3, 6	4
7	1, 7	2

b What kind of numbers have exactly two factors? _____

c What kind of numbers have exactly three factors? _____

2 Find the primes that are less than 100. More than 2000 years ago the Greek mathematician Eratosthenes devised a method for finding primes that is still used today. It is known as the sieve of Eratosthenes.

On this list of counting numbers up to 100, first cross out 1 (it is not prime).

- Neatly cross out all the multiples of 2 (all the even numbers) except 2, up to 100.
- Cross out all the multiples of 3, except 3, up to 99.
- Continue this process with the numbers 5 and 7.
- Circle all the remaining integers. You should now have circled all the primes between 1 and 100.

1	2	3	4	5	6	7	8	9	10
11	12	13	14	15	16	17	18	19	20
21	22	23	24	25	26	27	28	29	30
31	32	33	34	35	36	37	38	39	40
41	42	43	44	45	46	47	48	49	50
51	52	53	54	55	56	57	58	59	60
61	62	63	64	65	66	67	68	69	70
71	72	73	74	75	76	77	78	79	80
81	82	83	84	85	86	87	88	89	90
91	92	93	94	95	96	97	98	99	100

Prime patterns

1 **a** Use this table and the method of the sieve of Eratosthenes to find all the primes less than 100. Circle all the primes.

b Use your marking on the table to answer the following questions.

    i Which column has all the multiples of 6? _____

    ii Which column has all the numbers that are 1 more than a multiple of 6? _____

    iii Which two columns have all the primes except for 2 and 3? _____

    iv Complete this statement: 'Every prime number greater than 3 is 1 more or 1 less than a multiple of ...'. _____

A	B	C	D	E	F
1	2	3	4	5	6
7	8	9	10	11	12
13	14	15	16	17	18
19	20	21	22	23	24
25	26	27	28	29	30
31	32	33	34	35	36
37	38	39	40	41	42
43	44	45	46	47	48
49	50	51	52	53	54
55	56	57	58	59	60
61	62	63	64	65	66
67	68	69	70	71	72
73	74	75	76	77	78
79	80	81	82	83	84
85	86	87	88	89	90
91	92	93	94	95	96
97	98	99	100		

2 Use the method of the sieve of Eratosthenes in **a** and **b** below.

a Write the numbers from 1 to 100 in four columns and circle all the primes.

b Write these numbers in five columns and circle all the primes.

c What prime patterns can you discover in **a** _____ ?

d What prime patterns can you discover in **b** _____ ?

3 Complete this spiral of numbers and circle all the primes. Where are the square numbers?

_____

_____

_____

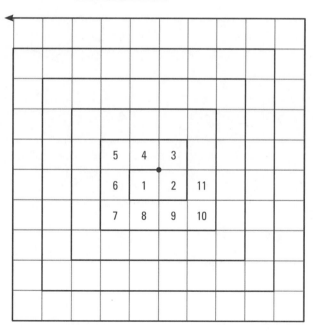

Goldbach's conjecture

A conjecture is a statement that seems true but for which there is as yet no proof.

In 1742, the German mathematician Goldbach made the conjecture that 'every even number greater than 4 is the sum of two prime numbers'. Even though thousands of even numbers have been tested and every one of them has been found to be the sum of two prime numbers, no one has been able to prove that every even number has this property.

10 = 7 + 3

Express each of these even numbers as the sum of two prime numbers by writing the prime numbers in the cubes.

1
2
3
4

5
6
7
8

9
10
11
12

13
14
15
16

17
18
19
20

Which number remains?

To complete the following, you must understand the following terms: *factors*, *multiples*, *primes* and *square numbers*.

In each question cross out what you are asked to and then circle the number that remains.

1 2, 3, 4, 6, 8, 12   Cross out all the factors of 12.

2 9, 12, 15, 16, 18   Cross out all the multiples of 3.

3 9, 49, 1, 81, 15, 25   Cross out all the odd square numbers.

4 8, 5, 12, 10, 6, 20   Cross out all the multiples of 4 and then cross out all the factors of 20.

5 2, 3, 4, 11, 15, 21   Cross out all the multiples of 3 and all the primes.

6 2, 5, 7, 11, 15, 25   Cross out all the factors of 25, and all the primes.

7 3, 6, 7, 14, 21, 28   Cross out all the factors of 21, and cross out all the multiples of 7.

8 4, 6, 15, 9, 16, 18   Cross out all the factors of 24, and cross out all the multiples of 3.

9 16, 25, 81, 45, 9, 36   Cross out all the square numbers.

10 3, 5, 6, 9, 15, 25   Cross out all the factors of 12, and cross out all the multiples of 5.

11 2, 3, 5, 6, 9, 12   Cross out all the factors of 15, and cross out all the factors of 18.

12 3, 5, 15, 25, 45, 9   Cross out all the factors of 45.

Arrange the numbers

1 Arrange the numbers 1 to 11 in the circles of the figure so that all three numbers in any line will give the same sum. There are three possible solutions. Can you find them all?

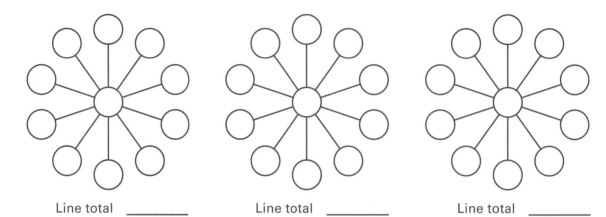

Line total _____   Line total _____   Line total _____

2 Arrange the numbers 1 to 8 in these squares so that each horizontal and vertical set forms a true statement.

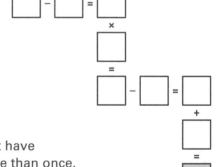

3 In these star patterns, all lines of numbers must have the same total and no number can be used more than once. Put numbers in the empty circles to make the total given.

a Total: 32   **b** Total: 24   **c** Total: 28

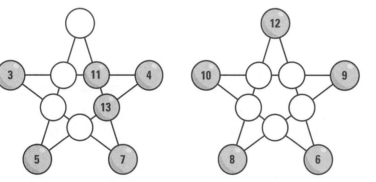

  4 Arrange four different digits in these boxes to make a true statement. There are numerous solutions to this problem. How many can you find? _____

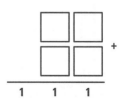

Triangle patterns

In this type of figure, the number in a square is always the sum of the numbers in the circles on either side of it.

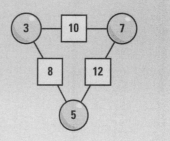

Find the numbers that fit in the circles in these diagrams.

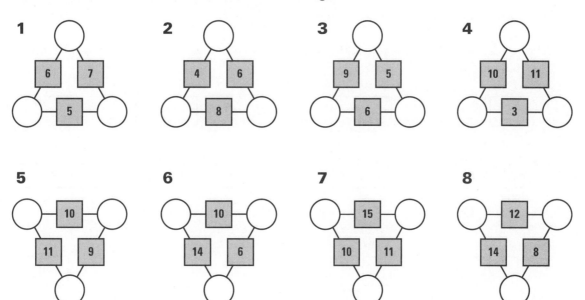

Have you found a quick way of doing these? In one of the problems you have solved, add the numbers in the squares, halve the answer, and look for the pattern with this number as a guide. Now try to solve the following examples using the shortcut.

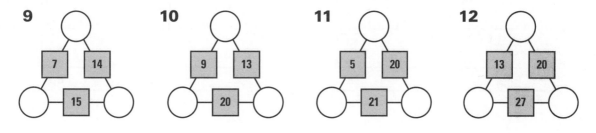

What's my question?

You will need to know your tables very well to solve these problems.

The question here is: 'What two numbers can I multiply together to give the answer 75?'

There are two possible answers to this question:

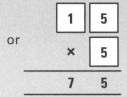

or

What questions must I ask to get the answers given below? Write down two different possibilities for each problem.

1

2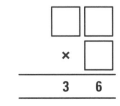

3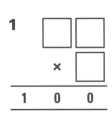

4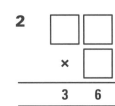

5

6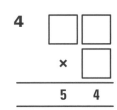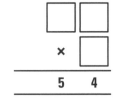

7

8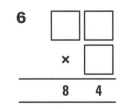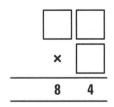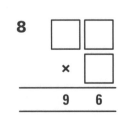

24

Dartboard problems

1 In one game of darts, 3 and 5 are the only possible scores in one throw.

    a What scores are possible? _____

    b What scores are impossible? _____

2 In another game of darts, 2 and 7 are the only possible values for a throw.

    a What scores are possible? _____

    b What scores are impossible? _____

3 Robert threw four darts at this dartboard and all four hit a target.

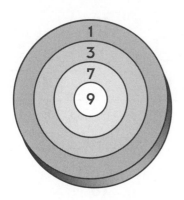

Which of the following numbers
could his total score have been?

  ◯ 17   ◯ 22

  ◯ 25   ◯ 18

  ◯ 24   ◯ 11

  ◯ 16   ◯ 31

4 In a game of darts in which 9, 6 and 2 are the only possible scores. Calculate:

    a the smallest number of
throws needed to score exactly 34; _____

    b the greatest number of
throws needed to score exactly 34. _____

    c Write down four different ways that a score of
18 can be achieved.

_____ _____ _____ _____

Missing digits

In these calculations, some of the digits are missing. Can you discover what these digits should be and write them in the boxes?

1
```
    □ 3
+   3 □
───────
    7 5
```

2
```
  1 3 □
+ □ □ 5
───────
  3 8 9
```

3
```
  4 □ 2
+ □ 6 □
───────
  7 4 7
```

4
```
  3 8 □
+ □ □ 5
───────
  9 7 6
```

5
```
  2 □ 4
+ □ 8 □
───────
  6 6 3
```

6
```
    7 □ 2
+   3 7 □
─────────
  □ □ 1 0
```

7
```
    7 8
−   □ □
───────
    5 4
```

8
```
    3 7 9
−   □ □ □
─────────
    1 5 2
```

9
```
    8 □
−   □ 4
───────
    5 3
```

10
```
    4 □
−   □ 8
───────
      4
```

11
```
    □ 2 □
−   2 □ 6
─────────
      3 8
```

12
```
    4 □ 2
−   □ 7 □
─────────
    2 5 3
```

13
```
    1 3
×     □
───────
    6 5
```

14
```
    6 □
×     3
─────────
  □ □ 7
```

15
```
    □ □
×     7
─────────
  3 7 8
```

16
```
    2 □ □
×       4
───────────
  □ 9 2
```

17
```
    2 □ □
×       4
───────────
  □ □ 9 2
```

18
```
    2 □ 6
×       □
───────────
    □ 3 8
```

19
```
    □ □ □
×       7
───────────
  2 5 5 5
```

20
```
    □ 7 □
×       9
───────────
  1 □ □ 3
```

Open-ended questions

1 The number 6 has four factors: 1, 2, 3, 6, while the number 11 has only two factors: 1 and 11. The factors of 24 are 1, 2, 3, 4, 6, 8, 3, 6, 12, 24.

   a Write down three numbers that have 3 and 2 as a factor. _____

   b Write down three numbers that have 5 and 2 as a factor. _____

   c List some counting numbers less than 30 that have exactly two different factors. _____

   d Write down some numbers that have the same number of factors as the following numbers: 25, 49 and 121

   _____

2 How many lollies are in the bag if:

   a a bag of lollies can be divided in equal shares among 2 friends or 3 friends; _____

   b a bag of lollies can be divided in equal shares among 3 friends or 4 friends; _____

   c a bag of lollies can be divided in equal shares among 2 friends, 3 friends or 4 friends; _____

   d a bag of lollies can be divided in equal shares among 2 friends and 5 friends. _____

3 I am thinking of a two-digit number. It is less than 40. The sum of its digits is 10. What number is it? _____

4 I am thinking of three different numbers. Their product is 24. What three numbers are they? _____

5 I am thinking of a two-digit square number. This number is divisible by 4. What number is it? _____

6 I am thinking of a two-digit prime number. Its unit digit is 1 (it ends in a 1). What number is it? _____

7 Find two or more fractions whose:

   a sum is 1 _____

   b sum is $\frac{5}{2}$ _____

   c difference is $\frac{3}{4}$ _____

   d product is 1. _____

What fraction's shaded?

Write down the fraction shaded in each diagram, and on the next diagram shade in another possible way illustrating the same fraction shaded.

1

 _____

2

 _____

3

 _____

4

 _____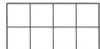

5

 _____

6

 _____

7

 _____

8

 _____

9

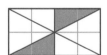 _____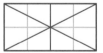

10

 _____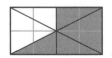

11

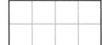 _____

12

Hexagon fractions

What fraction of the hexagon is shaded?

1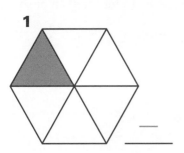

2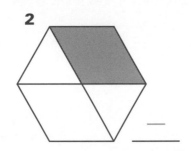

3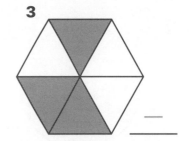

4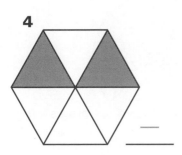

5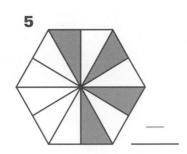

6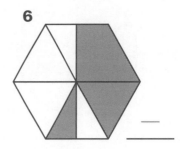

7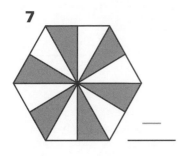

8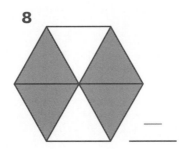

9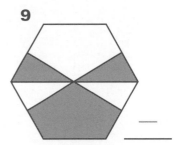

10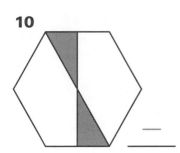

11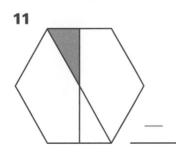

12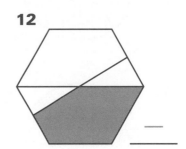

Pizza maths

Each diagram below represents a pizza. Jozef eats the fraction given in each question. Shade this amount and then write down how many pieces of pizza are left in each case.

1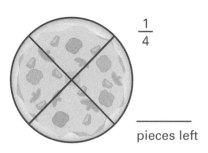
$\dfrac{1}{2}$

_____
pieces left

2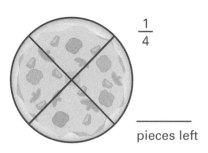
$\dfrac{1}{4}$

_____
pieces left

3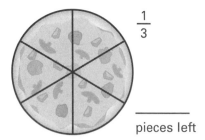
$\dfrac{1}{3}$

_____
pieces left

4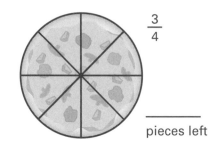
$\dfrac{3}{4}$

_____
pieces left

5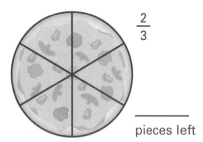
$\dfrac{2}{3}$

_____
pieces left

6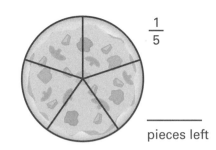
$\dfrac{1}{5}$

_____
pieces left

7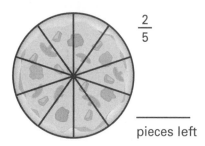
$\dfrac{2}{5}$

_____
pieces left

8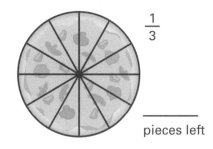
$\dfrac{1}{3}$

_____
pieces left

9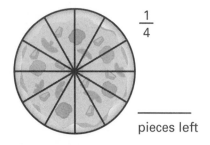
$\dfrac{1}{4}$

_____
pieces left

10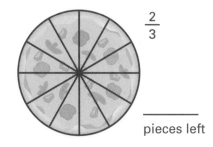
$\dfrac{2}{3}$

_____
pieces left

Problem-solving fractions

These problems can be solved easily if you use a diagram as shown below.

1   David had $200 in the bank. He bought a present for his mother for $\frac{1}{2}$ of this amount and spent $\frac{1}{2}$ of the remainder on some books.

How much does he have left? _____

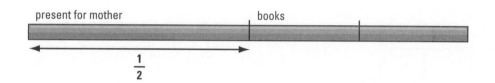

2   Eddie earned $250 last week. He bought food for $\frac{1}{5}$ of this amount and spent $\frac{1}{4}$ of the remaining rent.

How much does he have left? _____

3   Dylan had a sum of money. After he spent $\frac{1}{2}$ on a DVD, and he put $\frac{1}{2}$ of the remainder in the bank, he had $12 left.

How much money did Dylan have at the start? _____

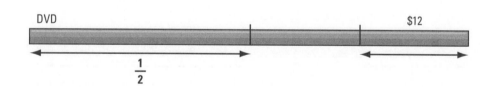

4   Romy had a sum of money. After she spent $\frac{1}{3}$ on a skirt, she went to the fun park and spent $\frac{1}{2}$ of the remainder. She had $20 left.

How much money did Romy have at the start? _____

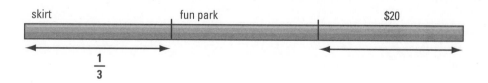

Problems with fractions

These problems can be solved easily if you use a diagram as shown below.

1 After Daniel spends $\frac{1}{5}$ of his money, he gives $\frac{1}{2}$ of what remains to Jordana. He now has $20 left.

How much did he start with? _____

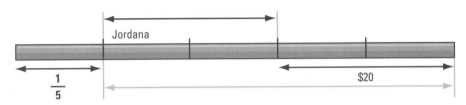

2 Lauren had a sum of money. After she spent $\frac{1}{2}$ at the movies and on lunch, she bought a CD with $\frac{1}{3}$ of the remainder. She had $12 left.

a How much money did Lauren spend on a CD? _____

b How much money did Lauren have at the start? _____

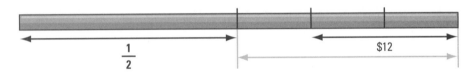

3 Matthew spent $\frac{1}{4}$ of his money on a computer game. Next he spent $\frac{1}{3}$ of the remainder at a concert. He has $40 remaining.

a How much money did Matthew spend at the concert? _____

b How much money did Matthew have at the start? _____

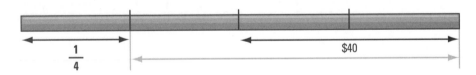

4 Lee spent $\frac{1}{3}$ of her money on a jacket. Next she spent $\frac{1}{4}$ of the remainder on a skirt. She has $360 remaining.

a How much money did Lee spend on the skirt? _____

b How much money did Lee have at the start? _____

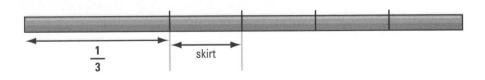

Number machine

Any number (1, 2, 3 and so on) can be fed into the number machine. One of two things will happen:

- if the input number is **even**, the machine will **divide the number by two**.
- if the input number is **odd**, the machine will **add one to it and divide the result by two**.

1 **a** If the input was 12, what was the output? _____

    b If the input was 11, what was the output? _____

    c If the output was 4, what are the two possible input numbers? _____

    d If the output was 7, what are the two possible input numbers? _____

2 Suppose you feed the output back into the input, continuing to do so until the output reaches 1.

If you start with an input of 11, you will get   11 ⟶ 6 ⟶ 3 ⟶ 2 ⟶ 1.

    a Write down the output at each stage if:

       i you start with an input of 19;

       _____

       ii you start with an input of 28.

       _____

    b In the example shown above, 3 is the third-last output. What are the two possible input numbers at:

       i one stage before the 3?

       ii two stages before the 3?

    Write your answers in the boxes.

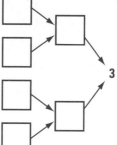

Where's the number?

1 Suppose all the counting numbers are written in columns in the pattern shown.

   a Continue the pattern for three more lines.

   b Name the letter of the column in which the number 28 appears. _____

   c Name the letter of the column in which the number 36 appears. _____

   d Name the letter of the column in which the number 34 appears. _____

   e Name the letter of the column in which the number 70 appears. _____

   f Name the letter of the column in which the number 71 appears. _____

L	M	N	O	P	Q	R
4		3		2		1
	5		6		7	
11		10		9		8
	12		13		14	

2 Suppose all the counting numbers are written in columns in the pattern shown.

   a Continue the pattern for three more lines.

   b Name the letter of the column in which the number 28 appears. _____

   c Name the letter of the column in which the number 35 appears. _____

   d Name the letter of the column in which the number 43 appears. _____

   e Name the letter of the column in which the number 70 appears. _____

   f Name the letter of the column in which the number 50 appears. _____

T	U	V	W	X	Y	Z
1	2	3	4	5	6	7
14	13	12	11	10	9	8
15	16	17	18	19	20	21
				24	23	22

Money problems

Use the guess and check method to solve these money problems.

1 A bottle of lemon drink costs $2. Find the value of the bottle in each case if:

   a the drink costs $1 more than the bottle: _____

   b the drink costs $1.20 more than the bottle: _____

   c the drink costs $1.50 more than the bottle. _____

2 Together a shirt and a tie cost $100. Find the cost of each if:

   a the shirt cost $20 more than the tie;   shirt _____ tie _____

   b the shirt cost $50 more than the tie;   shirt _____ tie _____

   c the shirt cost $90 more than the tie.   shirt _____ tie _____

3 Together a book and a pen cost $60. If the book cost $50 more than the pen, find the cost of each.   book _____ pen _____

4 Together Peter and Daniel spent $67 shopping. If Peter spent $3 more than Daniel, how much did each boy spend?

   Peter _____   Daniel _____

5 It costs 30c to mail a postcard and 40c to mail a letter. Lydia wrote to five friends and spent $1.60. How many postcards and how many letters did she write? Use a table to work out your solution.

Postcards (30c)	Letters (40c)	Total spent

6 Pencils cost 25c and sharpeners cost 40c. Emily bought twice as many pencils as sharpeners, and spent $2.70. How many pencils and how many sharpeners did she buy?

   _____ pencils   _____ sharpeners

7 Tamir has some 5c and 10c coins in his pocket. Work out how many coins of each value he has if they make a total of:

   a 60c, consisting of 10 coins   _____ 10c _____ 5c

   b 80c, consisting of 10 coins   _____ 10c _____ 5c

   c 70c, consisting of 12 coins   _____ 10c _____ 5c

   d $1.00 consisting of 12 coins.   _____ 10c _____ 5c

At the market

1 How many bananas can I get for the price of:

    a 4 apples? _____

    b 8 apples? _____

    c 2 kg pears? _____

    d 2 kg grapes? _____

2 How many mangoes can I get for the price of:

    a a punnet of strawberries? _____

    b 3 kg grapes? _____

3 What weight of pears can I get for the same price as:

    a 5 bananas? _____

    b 12 apples? _____

    c 2 punnets of strawberries? _____

    d 1 kg of grapes? _____

4 How many bananas would I get for the same price as:

    a 8 apples and 2 kg of grapes? _____

    b 8 mangoes? _____

5 If I got 4 kg of potatoes for the same price as
5 bananas, how much did a kilogram of potatoes cost? _____

Shopping

1 Nine cassettes cost $72. Find the cost of 4 cassettes. _____

2 Five apples cost $2.50. Find the cost of 9 apples. _____

3 Six tea towels cost $42. Find the cost of:

a 5 tea towels _____

b 9 tea towels. _____

4 If 7 pencils cost $2.80, how much will 2 pencils cost? _____

5 If 12 apples cost $3:

a How many apples can I buy for these amounts:

i 25c _____

ii $2.50 _____

iii 75c? _____

b Find the cost of:

i 5 apples _____

ii 9 apples _____

iii 30 apples. _____

6 **a** In a greengrocer's shop, 1 apple and 2 oranges cost $2.75, and 2 apples and 1 orange cost $3.25. Find the cost of:

i 3 apples and 3 oranges _____

ii 1 apple and 1 orange _____

iii 1 orange _____

iv 1 apple. _____

b At the same greengrocer's, 2 lemons and 3 pears cost $3.20, and 3 lemons and 2 pears cost $2.80.

Find the cost of:

i 5 lemons and 5 pears _____

ii 1 lemon and 1 pear _____

iii 2 lemons and 2 pears _____

iv 1 pear. _____

7 The cost of a drink and 3 sandwiches is $9.50. At the same prices, 2 drinks and 4 sandwiches cost $14.

How much does 1 drink cost? _____

Missing shapes

For each set of shapes or letters below, two more are needed to fill in the gap to complete the pattern. Can you work out what they are?

1

2

3

4

5

6

7   D A D B A D D A D B A ____ A D B A D

8   M M D C C D M ____ C C D M M D C C D

9

10

Halves and quarters

1 In each of these squares, one half has been shaded.

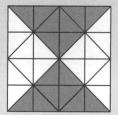 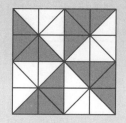 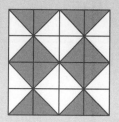

Can you shade one half of every square below to make eight different patterns?

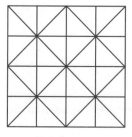 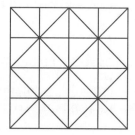 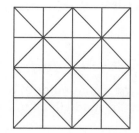 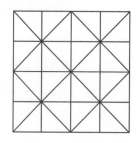

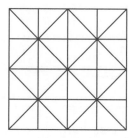 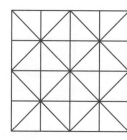 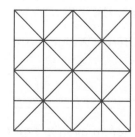 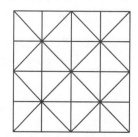

2 In these squares, one quarter has been shaded.

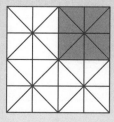 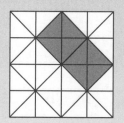 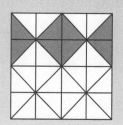

Can you shade one quarter of every square below to make four different patterns?

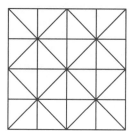 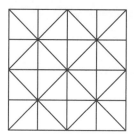 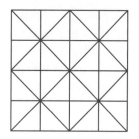 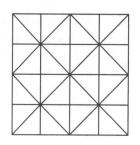

How many possibilities?

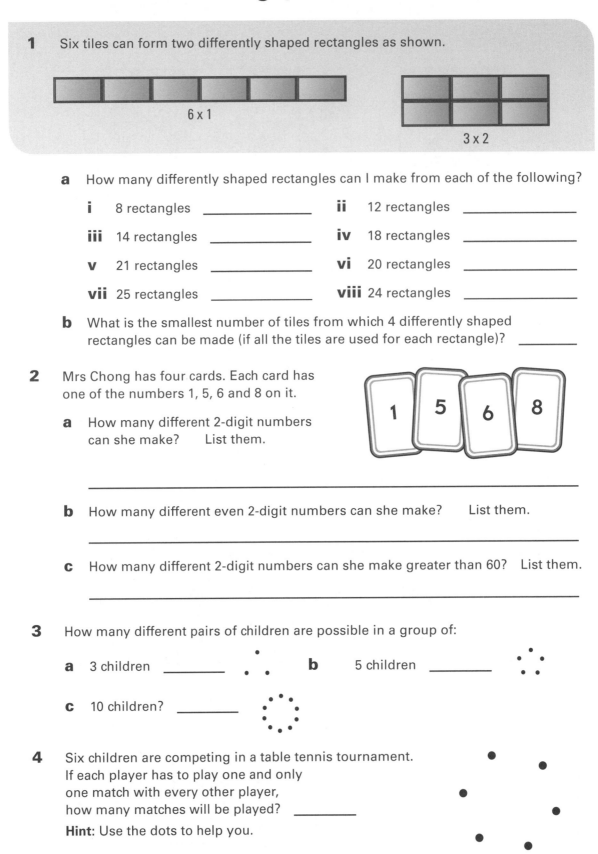

1 Six tiles can form two differently shaped rectangles as shown.

6 x 1

3 x 2

a How many differently shaped rectangles can I make from each of the following?

i 8 rectangles _____

ii 12 rectangles _____

iii 14 rectangles _____

iv 18 rectangles _____

v 21 rectangles _____

vi 20 rectangles _____

vii 25 rectangles _____

viii 24 rectangles _____

b What is the smallest number of tiles from which 4 differently shaped rectangles can be made (if all the tiles are used for each rectangle)? _____

2 Mrs Chong has four cards. Each card has one of the numbers 1, 5, 6 and 8 on it.

a How many different 2-digit numbers can she make? List them.

_____

b How many different even 2-digit numbers can she make? List them.

_____

c How many different 2-digit numbers can she make greater than 60? List them.

_____

3 How many different pairs of children are possible in a group of:

a 3 children _____

b 5 children _____

c 10 children? _____

4 Six children are competing in a table tennis tournament.
If each player has to play one and only
one match with every other player,
how many matches will be played? _____

Hint: Use the dots to help you.

Counting techniques

Using the digits 5 and 6, we can form two 2-digit numbers (56 and 65) if the digits cannot be repeated. However, if they can be repeated we can form these numbers:

55   65   56   66

1   Discover how many 2-digit numbers can be formed using 5, 6 and 7 if the digits:

   a   cannot be repeated _____

   b   can be repeated. _____

      _____

      List all the possibilities.

2   Work out how many 3-digit numbers can be formed using 5, 6 and 7 if the digits:

   a   cannot be repeated _____

   b   can be repeated. _____

      _____

3   How many 4-digit numbers can be formed using 5, 6, 7 and 8 if the digits cannot

   be repeated? _____

4   **a**   Glen has to number 27 seats for a concert by sticking the digits 0 to 9 on the seats. Therefore, for seat 23 he will need one digit 2 and one digit 3.

         i   How many digit 5s will he need? _____

         ii   How many digit 2s will he need? _____

         iii How many digit 0s will he need? _____

   b   Glenn now has to number 87 seats.

         i   How many digit 5s will he need? _____

         ii   How many digit 2s will he need? _____

         iii How many digit 0s will he need? _____

What chance?

1 In my class of 20 students, 10 students bring sandwiches for lunch, 5 bring a salad, 3 buy from the tuck shop and 2 eat fruit only. If a student is picked at random (without looking):

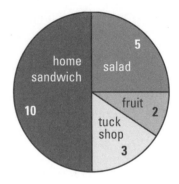

    a what is the chance that the person picked eats fruit only? _____

    b what did the student eat for lunch if there was 1 chance in 2 of that person being picked?

    _____

2 The diagram shows that the chance of picking a shaded rectangle is 1 in 3.

Shade rectangles to match the chance given in each question.

    a 1 in 5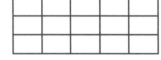

    b no chance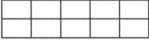

    c certain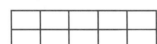

    d 1 in 4.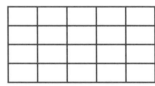

3 For every 12 Smarties in a packet, there are:
2 red, 1 blue, 3 yellow, 4 orange and 2 green.

    a If Jeremy counts 20 red Smarties, how many Smarties are there in his packet? _____

    b What is the chance that I pick a yellow Smartie from a packet? _____

    c If there is a 1 in 3 chance of picking a colour from a packet of Smarties, what colour is it? _____

    d If there are 60 Smarties in a packet, how many are blue? _____

    e Complete the graph on the right if there are 60 Smarties in a packet.

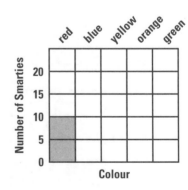

Spinner probabilities

Faye spins the pointers on these two spinners. She adds the numbers together to make a total.

A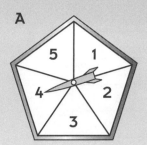

B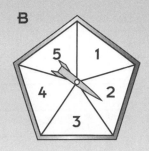

These two spinners have a total of 6.

Here is a table to show all the possible totals.

Number on Spinner B

		1	2	3	4	5
Number on Spinner A	**1**	2	3	4	5	6
	2	3	4	5	6	7
	3	4	5	6	7	8
	4	5	6	7	8	9
	5	6	7	8	9	10

Note that there are 25 possible outcomes. So the probability of getting a total of 2 is one chance in 25 or $\frac{1}{25}$.

Use the table to answer these questions.

1 What is the probability of getting a total of 4? _____

2 What is the probability of getting a total of 9? _____

3 What is the most likely total? _____

4 What is the probability of getting an even number as a total? _____

5 Which two totals are equally likely? _____

6 What is the probability of getting a total of 1? _____

7 What is the probability of getting a total greater than 7? _____

8 What is the probability of getting a total less than 4? _____

Picture graphs

1. This picture graph shows information on how teachers travel to a local school.

How teachers travel to school	
Train	🧍🧍🧍🧍🧍🧍🧍
Tram	🧍🧍🧍🧍
Taxi	🧍
Bus	🧍🧍🧍🧍🧍🧍🧍🧍
Car	🧍🧍🧍🧍🧍

Scale: 🧍 represents 5 teachers

   a If a person drawn represents five teachers,
      how many teachers travel to this school? _____

   b Which type of transport do most teachers use? _____

   c Which type of transport do least teachers use? _____

   d How many teachers travel to work by car? _____

   e By which type of transport do 20 teachers travel? _____

2. This picture graph shows the number of apples sold at the school canteen during one week.

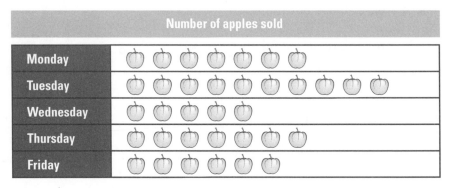

Scale: 🍎 represents 3 apples

   a How many apples were sold on Wednesday? _____

   b On which day were the same number of apples sold? _____

   c How many apples were sold on both these days? _____

   d On which day were the most number of apples sold? _____

   e How many apples were sold altogether during the week? _____

Picture this

These graphs give us information by means of pictures.

1   This picture graph shows the number of children who bought various items at the canteen during recess.

Each 𝀂 represents three children, and each child bought only one item.

   a   How many children bought a drink? _____

   b   How many children bought an ice-block? _____

   c   How many children bought a piece of cake? _____

   d   Which item was the most popular? _____

       How many children bought it? _____

   e   Which item was the least popular? _____

       How many children bought it? _____

   f   Altogether, how many children were served during recess? _____

   g   If 15 sandwiches were prepared, how many were left over? _____

2   This picture graph shows the number of balls sold in one week by a sports store.

Each 🎾 represents four balls.

   a   How many of each of these balls were sold?

       i   tennis balls _____

       ii   footballs _____

       iii   basketballs _____

       iv   golf balls _____

   b   How many balls were sold altogether? _____

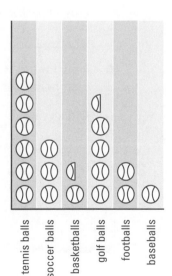

Graphs

1 Draw a picture graph to show the number of hours of television each of the following children watch during a week of the school holidays.

Use a scale of 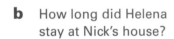 to represent 4 hours.

	George	Emanuel	Laura	Phoebe	Mimi
Time spent watching TV in hours	20	16	24	8	12

Draw the required number of symbols beside each name in the grid.

Time spent watching TV					
George					
Emanuel					
Laura					
Phoebe					
Mimi					

2 The graph shows Helena's position from her home during a walk to visit two friends.

a Her first stop is to visit Nick at his home. How far does Nick live from Helena?

_____

b How long did Helena stay at Nick's house?

_____

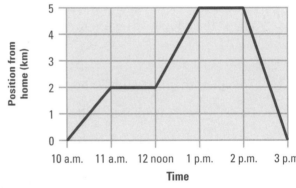

c How far did Helena travel to visit her second friend, George? _____

d Did she travel faster or slower to George's house? _____

3 On Friday 120 students used the school canteen. The number of students from each year group was recorded and displayed in the bar chart below.

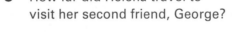

a How many Year 3 students went to the canteen on Friday? _____

b How many Year 5 students went to the canteen on Friday? _____

Sector graph

The graph below shows how Joe spent his leisure time in a week.

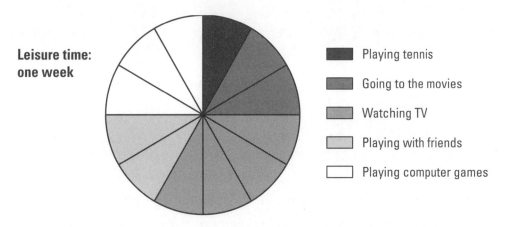

Leisure time: one week

- ■ Playing tennis
- ■ Going to the movies
- ■ Watching TV
- ■ Playing with friends
- □ Playing computer games

1   If he had 24 hours of leisure time, how much time did Joe spend:

   a   playing tennis   _____

   b   playing with friends?   _____

2   If he spent 3 hours playing tennis, how many hours did he spend:

   a   watching TV   _____

   b   going to the movies   _____

   c   on leisure activities altogether?   _____

3   If Joe was on school holidays with 60 hours of
leisure time in a week, how many hours did he spend:

   a   playing tennis   _____

   b   playing computer games   _____

   c   watching TV?   _____

Perimeter

1 The perimeter of a shape is the distance around the figure. It is the sum of the lengths of the sides.

Three rectangles can be drawn with perimeters of 8 cm, if one side is horizontal and measurements are only in whole numbers.

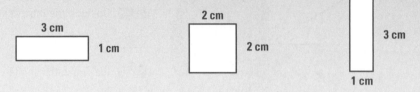

Find the number of rectangles that can be drawn for each perimeter given.

Use squared paper to illustrate each perimeter that you consider, then complete this table.

Perimeter (in cm)	Possible rectangles
8	3
10	
12	
14	
16	

2 To find the perimeter of this figure, you will first have to work out the lengths that are not given. All measurements are in centimetres.

The unmarked horizontal side must be 4 cm, because 4 + 6 = 10. *Similarly*, you can show that the unmarked vertical length is 5 cm, because 5 + 3 = 8.

Therefore, the perimeter of the figure is 36 cm.

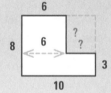

Find the perimeter of each of the following figures. (All lines are either horizontal or vertical and are given in cm.)

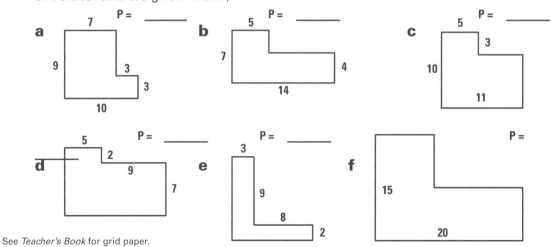

See *Teacher's Book* for grid paper.

48

Find the perimeter

1   Find the perimeter of the following figures, assuming that they are drawn on 1 cm grid paper. What properties do all the figures in **a** and all the figures in **b** have in common? On squared paper, draw three other shapes having the common property in **a** and three shapes with the common property in **b**.

a

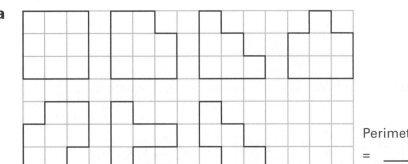

Perimeter
= _____

b

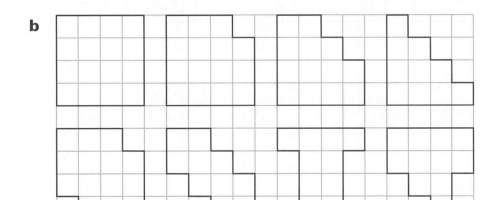

Perimeter = _____

2   Now try this interesting problem. Explain your result.

Alan and his sister, Diane, walk to school each day, but Diane knows a shortcut.

If the children leave home at the same time and walk at the same speed, who will get to school first?

_____

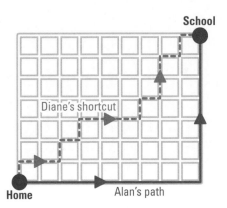

Area investigation

If this square ▢ is one square unit,

then this shaded triangle ◿ has an area of $\frac{1}{2}$ square unit,

while this shaded triangle △ has an area of 1 square unit.

1 Which of the shaded figures below have an area of 2 square units?

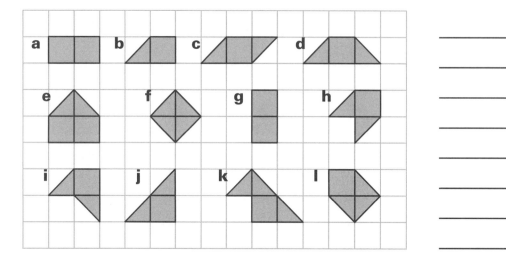

_____

_____

_____

_____

_____

_____

_____

2 Using the squared paper:

a draw some shapes with an area of 3 square units.

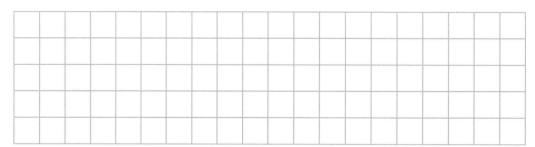

b draw some shapes with an area of 4 square units.

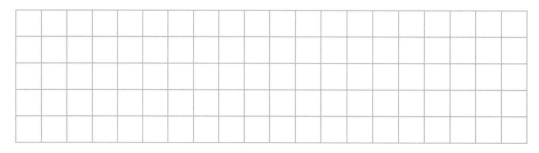

Perimeter and area

The *perimeter* of a figure is the distance around it.

The *area* of a figure is the amount of surface enclosed by it.

This figure has a perimeter of 12 units and an area of 6 square units.

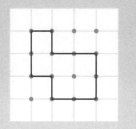

In the table below, the perimeters and the areas of figures are given.

Draw each of these figures using the dots and squared paper below.

The sides of all figures must be horizontal or vertical.

(*There are a few solutions to **d** and many solutions to **f**.)

	Perimeter (units)	Area (square units)
a	4	1
b	6	2
c	8	4
d	10	4*
e	10	5
f	12	5*
g	10	6
h	12	8
i	12	9
j	16	16

Taping boxes

1   A piece of tape is wrapped all the way round a box exactly once as shown.

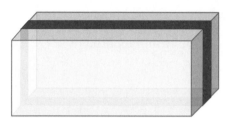

a   If the length of the box is 20 cm and the height is 8 cm,
then show that the tape is 56 cm.   _____ = 56

b   If the length of the box is 18 cm and the
height is 7 cm, find the length of the tape.   _____

c   If the length of the box is 15 cm and the
tape is 50 cm long, find the height of the box.   _____

d   If the length of the box is 25 cm and the
tape is 60 cm long, find the height of the box.   _____

2   This time a piece of tape is wrapped all the way round a box in both directions
exactly once as shown.

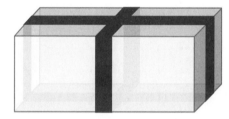

a   If the length of the box is 20 cm, the width is 6 cm and the height 8 cm,
then show that the tape is 84 cm. Check carefully how the tape is wrapped and
write down what calculation needs to be done to get this answer.

_____

_____

_____

b   If the length of the box is 18 cm, the width is 7 cm
and the height is 5 cm, find the length of the tape.   _____

c   If the length of the box is 15 cm and the width is 5 cm,
find the height of the box if the tape is 100 cm long.   _____

d   If the length of the box is 24 cm and the width is 12 cm,
find the height of the box if the tape is 100 cm long.   _____

Measurement

Show the temperature

Show the temperature indicated on each of the following thermometers.

Carefully study the scale before you attempt each question.

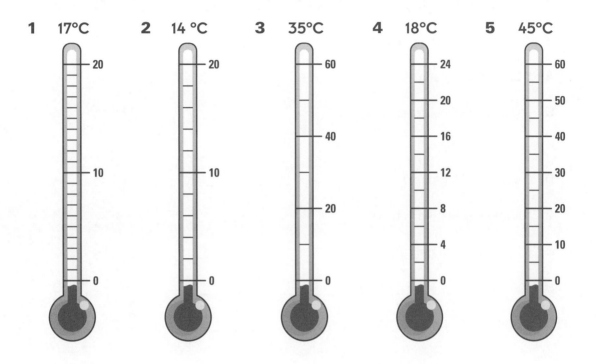

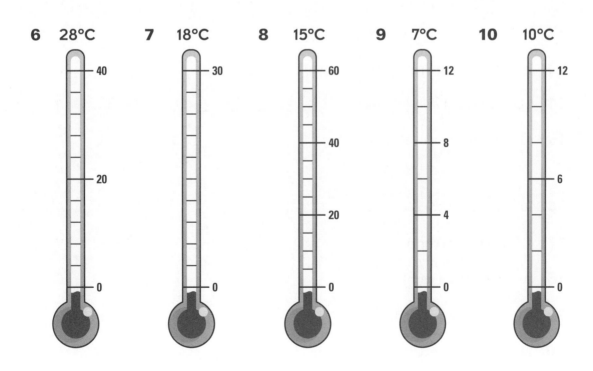

Match the answer

Work out the total quantity and write the correct letter to match the measure.

1	10 stamps at 50 cents each	_____	$6	A
2	5 lollies at 20 cents each	_____	$2	B
3	100 stickers at 4 cents each	_____	$5	C
4	3 books at $2 each	_____	$4	D
5	20 rules at 10 cents each	_____	$1	E

6	3 apples (250 g each)	_____	1 kg	A
7	10 boxes (500 g each box)	_____	6 kg	B
8	5 bananas (200 g each)	_____	5 kg	C
9	100 strawberries (30 g each)	_____	750 g	D
10	4 melons ($1\frac{1}{2}$ kg each)	_____	3 kg	E

11	10 cans of drink (375 mL each)	_____	3 L	A
12	4 containers of juice (3 L each)	_____	2·5 L	B
13	10 packets of apple juice (250 mL each)	_____	10 L	C
14	5 containers of milk (2 L each)	_____	3·75 L	D
15	5 bottles of cordial (600 mL each)	_____	12 L	E

16	10 ribbons (40 cm each)	_____	9·5 m	A
17	4 rulers (30 cm each)	_____	10 m	B
18	20 steps (50 cm each)	_____	4 m	C
19	10 jumps of 95 cm each	_____	14·5 m	D
20	10 rods (1.45 m each)	_____	1·2 m	E

Measurement using tables

To answer these questions, draw up tables and use guess and check.

1   Find the mass of each item in my shopping bag if:

    a   their total mass is 1 kg and the difference of their masses is 100 g; _____

    b   their total mass is 1·2 kg and the difference of their masses is 500 g. _____

2   Michelle and her younger sister, Mia, bought their mother a bracelet for her birthday. If Michelle decided to contribute twice as much as Mia and the bracelet cost $24, how much did each girl pay?

    Michelle _____   Mia _____

3   The total mass of three children is 35 kg. The oldest, Imran, is twice the mass of the youngest, Bruce. Gordon's mass is 3 kg more than Bruce's. Find Imran's mass.

Imran	Bruce	Gordon

4   Lemon drops come in packages of 3 for 20c. Chocolate mints cost 5c each. Tom bought 20 sweets and spent $1.20. How many of each kind did he buy?

Lemon drops (3)	Chocolate mints	Total spent

5   Bananas cost $3 for 1 kg and grapes cost $4 for 1 kg. How many kilograms of each did Mrs Morgan buy if:

    a   she spent $18 and had 5 kg of fruit;

    b   she spent $12? (give as many possible solutions as you can: part kilogram answers are acceptable)

	Bananas	Grapes	Cost
a			
b			

Fractions in measurement

1 If 1 kg of strawberries cost $12:

   a what would 250 grams cost? _____

   b how much did I buy if I spent $21? _____

2 A bottle of cough mixture is $\frac{1}{2}$ full. When 50 mL is used,
the container becomes $\frac{1}{4}$ full. Find the capacity of the container. _____

3 At a certain time of day the shadow cast is $1\frac{1}{2}$ times the actual height of the object.

   a How high is the tree if the shadow is 300 cm? _____

   b If Ben is 120 cm tall, how long is his shadow? _____

4 When full, Nathan's petrol tank can hold 48 litres of petrol.
He fills the tank when it is $\frac{1}{4}$ full.

   a How many litres are needed to fill the tank? _____

   b If petrol is $1.50 a litre, how much will it cost to fill up the tank? _____

   c If his car uses 1 litre of petrol for every 11 kilometres,
how far can Nathan travel on a full tank? _____

5 **a** Kate and Melissa share a 400 mL bottle of juice. If Kate drinks $\frac{3}{5}$
of the bottle, what amount of the juice remains for Melissa? _____

   b Luke and Samuel share a 600 mL bottle of juice. If Luke drinks $\frac{2}{3}$
of the bottle, what amount of the juice remains for Samuel? _____

6 If 2 kg of apples cost $10, what would:

   a 500 g cost? _____   **b** 750 g cost? _____

   c 5 kg cost? _____

7 Jim spent 2 hours at the beach. If he spent $\frac{3}{4}$ of that time
swimming and the rest playing with friends
on the sand, how long was he in the water? _____

Questioning time

1 George's radio alarm comes on at 20 to 7 in the morning. It is 6:28 on the digital clock when George wakes up.
How many more minutes till his alarm rings? _____

2 Marc leaves home at 7:55 a.m. and arrives at school at 8:23 a.m. How long did he take to get there? _____

3 Nicky left home at 6:22 a.m. (she had band practice), and returned home at 4:08 p.m. that afternoon.
How many hours and minutes was she away from home? _____

4 Mrs Ho gets up every morning at 6:30 a.m.

a If she went to bed on Thursday at 10:30 p.m., for how many hours was she awake? _____

b If on Friday she was awake for $12\frac{1}{2}$ hours, when did she go to bed that night? _____

5 Douglas left home at 7:20 a.m. and returned home at 6:50 p.m. For how long was he away from home? _____

6 Each day Mr Lee spends 8 hours 20 minutes at work.
How much time does he spend at work in 5 days? _____

7 A clock is set at 9 a.m. Since then it loses 10 seconds for every minute that passes. When the actual time is 10 a.m., what does the clock show? _____

8 A clock is set correctly at 1:00 p.m. If it loses 5 minutes every hour, what will the clock show when the correct time is 10:00 p.m. the same day? _____

9 A clock is set correctly at 1:00 p.m. If it loses 2 minutes every hour, what will the clock show when the correct time is 7:00 p.m. the same day? _____

10 A clock is set correctly at 1:00 p.m. If it loses 2 minutes every hour, what will the clock show when the correct time is 1:00 p.m. the next day? _____

Time challenges

1   Suppose four days before yesterday was Tuesday. What day will it be tomorrow?

_____

2   If 25 May 2005 occurred on a Wednesday, on which day of the week did:

a   11 May 2005 occur?   _____

b   9 May 2005 occur?   _____

c   3 June 2005 occur?   _____

3   Jennifer's birthday is the 23rd of April.

April						
Sunday	**Monday**	**Tuesday**	**Wednesday**	**Thursday**	**Friday**	**Saturday**
			1	2	3	4
5	6	7	8	9	10	11
12	13	14	15	16	17	18
19	20	21	22	23	24	25
26	27	28	29	30		

a   If today is the 29th of March, how many more days until her birthday?

_____

b   Jennifer's birthday party will be on the 2nd of May.

i   What day of the week will it be?   _____

ii   For how many days after her birthday will Jennifer have to wait until her party?   _____

c   If Alex, her brother, is 6 years and 8 months on Jennifer's birthday, what is Alex's age in months?   _____

d   If Jennifer is going to be 9 years old, what is the difference in age between them in months?   _____

4   Kylie had a piano lesson and tennis lesson on Monday.
She has piano lessons every four days and tennis lessons every three days.
On what day of the week will she next have both lessons on the same day?

_____

5   Sam has drama lessons every two weeks and swimming practice every four days.
If Sam had a drama lesson and swimming practice today, how long will it take before both occur on the same day again?

_____

Multiple choice—measurement

Colour in the bubble(s) next to the answer. (There may be more than one correct answer.)

1 A magazine has a mass of 250 g. A puzzle book has a mass of 300 g. What is the mass of two magazines and three puzzle books?

    A ◯ 1400 g   **B** ◯ 550 g   **C** ◯ 1·4 kg   **D** ◯ 1350 g

2 A book has a mass that is twice as much as a magazine. If a book has a mass of 400 g, what is the mass of two books and five magazines?

    A ◯ 1400 g   **B** ◯ 1800 g   **C** ◯ 2800 g   **D** ◯ 1.8 kg

3 A piece of string is 1 m long. It is cut into pieces that are each 10 cm long. Into how many pieces is it cut?

    A ◯ 1000   **B** ◯ 10   **C** ◯ 9   **D** ◯ 100

4 Each time Nick's phone rings, it rings for 4 seconds, then it is silent for 2 seconds. If Nick's phone rings two times, how much time does it take from the beginning of the first ring until the end of the final ring?

    A ◯ 10 seconds   **B** ◯ 12 seconds   **C** ◯ 8 seconds   **D** ◯ 6 seconds

5 How many grams in $\frac{1}{4}$ kg?

    A ◯ 25 g   **B** ◯ 205 g   **C** ◯ 2500 g   **D** ◯ 250 g

6 A cup holds 200 millilitres and a jug holds 1·5 litres. How many full cups can be filled from this jug?

    A ◯ 7   **B** ◯ 8   **C** ◯ 0   **D** ◯ 6

7 1 litre of water measures:

    A ◯ 1 kg   **B** ◯ 100 g   **C** ◯ 1000 g   **D** ◯ 10 g

8 The length of an average banana is closest to:

    A ◯ 0·17 m   **B** ◯ 0·25 m   **C** ◯ 17 cm   **D** ◯ 170 mm

9 In my shopping bag I have two 250 g tins of corn, 500 g of margarine, and a 750 g box of cereal. What is the total mass of groceries?

    A ◯ 1500 g   **B** ◯ $1\frac{3}{4}$ kg   **C** ◯ 1750 g   **D** ◯ $1\frac{1}{2}$ kg

10 If 14 March is a Monday, what day of the week will 14 April be?

    A ◯ Thursday   **B** ◯ Monday   **C** ◯ Tuesday   **D** ◯ Wednesday

11 How many metres in $2\frac{1}{2}$ kilometres?

    A ◯ 250 m   **B** ◯ 2500 m   **C** ◯ 25 000 m   **D** ◯ 2050 m

12 How many grams in $1\frac{1}{4}$ kg?

    A ◯ 1025 g   **B** ◯ 1250 g   **C** ◯ 125 g   **D** ◯ 10 025 g

Measurement problems

Colour in the bubble next to the correct answer. There could be more than one solution to some of these problems.

1 One of these clocks is 10 minutes slow and the other is 5 minutes fast. Find the correct time.

A ◯ 12:25   B ◯ 12:20

C ◯ 12:10   D ◯ 12:35

2 If 1 kilogram of jelly beans cost $16, what would 250 grams of jelly beans cost?

A ◯ $4   B ◯ $8   C ◯ $40   D ◯ $3

3 The perimeter of this rectangle is 96 m. Find its width.

27 m

A ◯ 42 m   B ◯ 21 m   C ◯ 69m   D ◯ 2100 cm

4 A comfortable temperature on a nice day is:

A ◯ 40°C   B ◯ 0°C   C ◯ 8°C   D ◯ 20°C

5 Joe is 12 years old. His mother is three times as old as he is. How old will he be when his mother turns 50?

A ◯ 24   B ◯ 26   C ◯ 38   D ◯ 36

6 Anthony wakes up at 6:40 a.m., takes 35 minutes to get dressed, 12 minutes to eat breakfast and 14 minutes to walk to school. At what time does he get to school?

A ◯ 7:01 a.m.   B ◯ 7:31 a.m.   C ◯ 7:51 a.m.   D ◯ 7:41 a.m.

7 The number of cents in 13 dollars and 8 cents is:

A ◯ 138   B ◯ 13 008   C ◯ 1308   D ◯ 1380

8 An average apple has a mass of about 140 grams. How many average apples make a mass of about 1 kilogram?

A ◯ 7   B ◯ 6   C ◯ 70   D ◯ 20

9 What is the maximum number of cards measuring 4 cm by 5 cm that can be cut from a piece of cardboard 20 cm by 24 cm?

A ◯ 24   B ◯ 21

C ◯ 18   D ◯ 20

4 cm
5 cm
20 cm
24 cm

10 What is the reading shown on the scale?

A ◯ 60 g   B ◯ 550 g

C ◯ 6000 g   D ◯ 600 g

0   1
kg

11 After a cataract operation Mr Koutes has to put three drops in his eye every 6 hours. How long would a bottle containing 96 drops last him?

A ◯ 8 days   B ◯ 16 days   C ◯ 32 days   D ◯ 6 days

Measurement

Packing cans

1   Cans are packed in boxes. Each can is 12 cm high and has a radius of 5 cm.
Find the length, width and height of each box.

a   There are 6 cans in this box as shown.

l = _____ cm

w = _____ cm

h = _____ cm

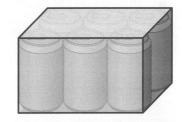

b   There are 18 cans in this box as shown.

l = _____ cm

w = _____ cm

h = _____ cm

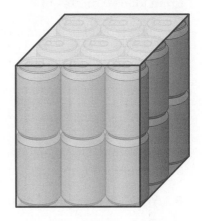

2   This container is 40 cm long, 30 cm wide
and 24 cm high. What is the most
number of the above cans that
can be placed inside this box?

_____

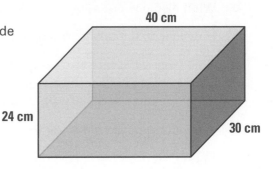

3   Twelve cans have to fit inside a box.

How many different ways can you pack the cans. Continue to list these and find the
size of each box. (All the measurements are in centimetres.)

Ways that cans are packed	length	width	height
12 x 1 x 1	120	10	12
6 x 2 x 1	60	20	12
4 x 3 x 1			
3 x 2 x 2			
2 x 2 x 3			

Speed challenges

1 Sarah walks 25 metres in 20 seconds. If she walks at the same speed:

    a How far will she walk in 4 minutes? _____

    b How far will she walk in 1 hour? _____

    c How long will it take her to walk 150 metres? _____

    d How long will it take her to walk 3 kilometres? _____

2 Brian jogs 20 metres in 12 seconds. If he jogs at the same speed:

    a How far will he jog in 4 minutes? _____

    b How far will he jog in 1 hour? _____

    c How long will it take him to jog 200 metres? _____

    d How long will it take him to jog 1 kilometre? _____

3 If a car is travelling at an average speed of 90 kilometres per hour (that is, 90 kilometres in 1 hour):

    a What distance does it cover in $2\frac{1}{2}$ hours? _____

    b What distance does it cover in 20 minutes? _____

    c How long will it take to travel 360 kilometres? _____

    d How long will it take to travel 150 kilometres? _____

4 If a car is travelling at an average speed of 84 kilometres per hour:

    a What distance does it cover in $1\frac{1}{2}$ hours? _____

    b What distance does it cover in 15 minutes? _____

    c How long will it take to travel 168 kilometres? _____

    d How long will it take to travel 63 kilometres? _____

Rate problems

1 While resting, Fiona can breathe 6 litres of air per minute.

While exercising, Ben can breathe 80 litres of air per minute.

a How much air will Fiona breathe in 5 minutes? _____

b How much air will Ben breathe in 5 minutes? _____

c How much more air will Ben breathe than Fiona in 5 minutes?

_____

2 If Kathleen's heart beats 70 times a minute:

a How many times does it beat in 1 hour? _____

b How long will it take to beat 2800 times? _____

3 William can swim 100 metres in $2\frac{1}{2}$ minutes.

a How far can he swim in 10 minutes? _____

b How far can he swim in 1 minute? _____

c How long will it take him to swim 10 metres? _____

4 Jeremy earns $18 per hour in his job.

a How much will he earn in 10 minutes? _____

b How much will he earn in 1 minute? _____

c How much will he earn in 5 hours? _____

d How long will it take Jeremy to earn $360? _____

5 Marc is a house painter who can paint walls at a rate of 30 m² per hour.

a How long will it take Marc to paint 240 m²? _____

b How long will it take Marc to paint 75 m²? _____

c What area of wall can Marc paint in 20 minutes? _____

d What area of wall can Marc paint in 4 minutes? _____

Water flow

1 Every minute, 20 litres of water flow into an empty pool. How many litres are in the pool after 1 hour? _____

2 The graph shows the number of litres of water flowing from two hoses.

a In 10 seconds, how much water flows from:

i the small hose?

_____

ii the large hose?

_____

b How many seconds does it take to fill a 300 litre tank using the small hose?

_____

c How many litres of water flow from the large hose in 5 seconds?

_____

d In 20 seconds, how much more water flows from the large hose than the small hose? _____

3 A bath fills at a rate of 4 litres every 12 seconds.

a How much water is in the bath after 1 minute? _____

b If Margaret fills the bath for 6 minutes, how much water is used? _____

4 Grace has a faulty tap and it drips at a rate of 3 mL per second. How much water is wasted in:

a a minute? _____

b an hour? _____

5 Rodney's tap drips at the rate of 5 mL every 12 seconds. How much water is wasted in 1 hour?

_____

Cough medicine

A full bottle of cough medicine contains 250 mL.

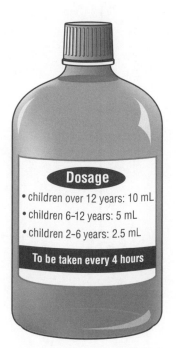

Heidi is 9 years old and her mum has just bought this bottle of cough mixture.

Heidi needs to take some every day from 6 a.m. till 10 p.m., every 4 hours.

1   How many times will she take it a day?   _____

2   In millilitres what is the dose for a 9 year old?   _____

3   How many millilitres will Heidi take a day?   _____

4   In a full bottle how many doses are
there for a 9 year-old child?   _____

5   For how many days will the medicine last,
if Heidi continues to take it till the bottle finishes?   _____

6   How much medicine will remain in the bottle after 4 days?   _____

7   If Heidi took the first dose on a Tuesday at 6 p.m.,
carefully work out when she will take the last dose.   _____

8   If the bottle of Heidi's cough mixture cost $15, how much
does it cost each day that she takes this medicine?   _____

Travel graphs

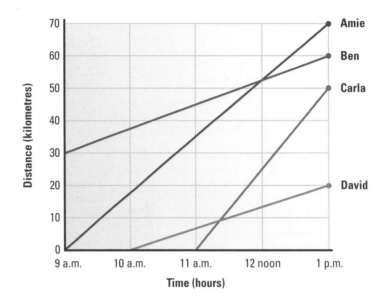

The graph above shows the travel of four people on Sunday between 9 a.m. and 1 p.m.

1 Who travelled the furthest in that time? _____

2 Which person travelled 50 km? _____

3 Which two people travelled for the same length of time?

_____   _____

4 David travelled 20 km. How long did he take to do that? _____

5 To work out the speed of travel we use the formula.   speed $= \dfrac{distance}{time}$

Work out Carla's speed. _____

6 Whose speed was greater Ben's, or Amie's? Give reasons for your answer by working out both their speeds.

Ben's _____   Amie's _____

7 Melanie left home (0 km) at 10 a.m., travelled to visit her friend 40 km away arriving at 12 noon. She then stayed at her friend's house till 1 p.m. Illustrate this on your graph.

Marbles

Steve fills two cylinders with the same amount of water and drops marbles into each cylinder. If the marbles are identical (exactly the same), in each question, find the volume of one marble and the amount of water in the cylinder before the marbles were placed in it.

1

240 mL  255 mL

Volume of
one marble = _____

Volume of
water = _____

2

240 mL  256 mL

Volume of
one marble = _____

Volume of
water = _____

3

240 mL  272 mL

Volume of
one marble = _____

Volume of
water = _____

4

340 mL  460 mL

Volume of
one marble = _____

Volume of
water = _____

Fuel tank

The two diagrams show the petrol gauge of a car before and after a trip. Find how many litres were used in each trip. The capacity of each car's fuel tank is given in each case.

1   40 L

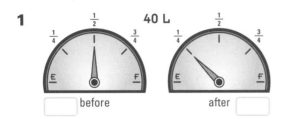

before   after

_____

2   80 L

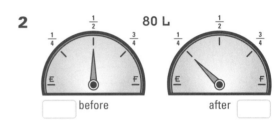

before   after

_____

3   60 L

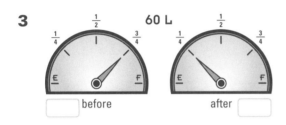

before   after

_____

4   32 L

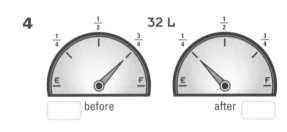

before   after

_____

5   48 L

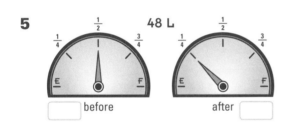

before   after

_____

6   56 L

before   after

_____

7   36 L

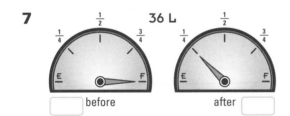

before   after

_____

8   24 L

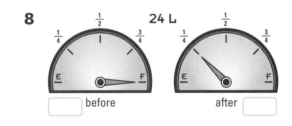

before   after

_____

Mass

Remember: 1000 g = 1 kg

1 Find the sum of 780 g and 650 g. _____

2 From 3 kg take 875 g. _____

3 How many 5 kg bags of potatoes are there in a sack holding 120 kg? _____

4 Find the total mass of a sack of carrots
if it holds 35 bags each weighing 4 kg. _____

5 From a case of 5 kg of strawberries,
how many 250 g punnets can we make? _____

6 From a case of 9 kg of cherries,
how many 450 g bags can we make? _____

7 How many 250 g tubs of margarine would have a total mass of 12 kg? _____

8 How many 375 g tubs of margarine would have a total mass of 3.75 kg? _____

9 If a can weighs 400 g, find the total mass of eight of these cans. _____

10 Paul has exactly eight small weights with a total mass of 50 grams.
The weights have a mass of 5 grams or 10 grams.
How many 5 gram weights does Paul have? _____

11 To find the average weight of a number of people, we add their weight and divide
by the total number of people.

a Find the average weight of three boys,
if their individual masses are 33 kg, 28 kg and 35 kg. _____

b If the average weight of three boys is 36 kg, and one weighs 38 kg
and another weighs 30 kg, what is the mass of the third boy? _____

12 I buy six cans of dog food, each weighing 500 g. When I weigh myself while
carrying the dog food, the scales read 46 kg. How much do I weigh?

_____

13 One kilogram of fish costs $16. What is the price of:

a 500 g? _____

b 750 g? _____

c 1500 g? _____

d 1250 g? _____

How many?

In these exercises, be sure to work systematically, counting small, medium and large shapes as required. You can shade the squares and triangles as you count them.

1 What is the total number of squares in each of these figures?

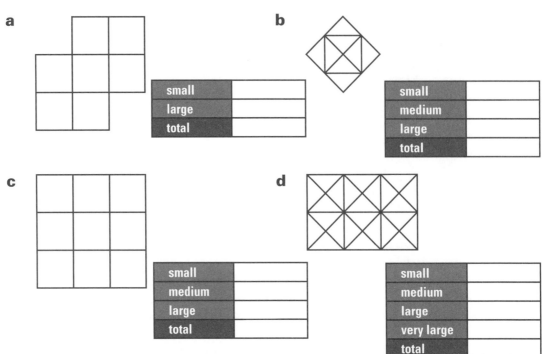

a

small	
large	
total	

b

small	
medium	
large	
total	

c

small	
medium	
large	
total	

d

small	
medium	
large	
very large	
total	

2 How many triangles can you find in each of these figures?

a

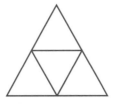

small	
large	
total	

b

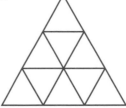

small	
medium	
large	
total	

c

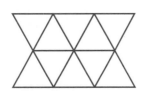

small	
medium	
total	

d

small	
medium	
large	
total	

See *Teacher's Book* for diagram masters.

Amazing graphs

Carefully copy the shape of the dog on the grids below.

Colour in the pictures you make.

Then design some different grids yourself and copy the dog on them.

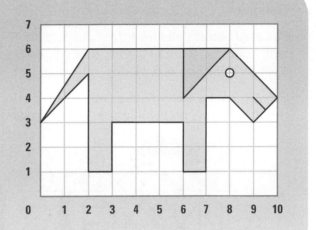

1

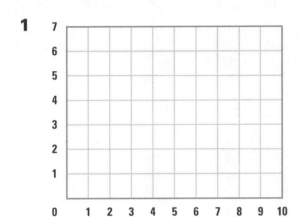

2

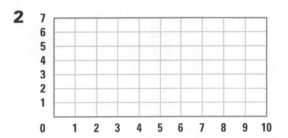

3

4

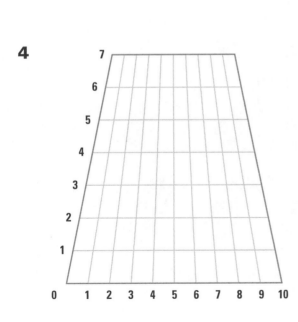

5

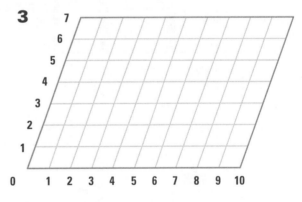

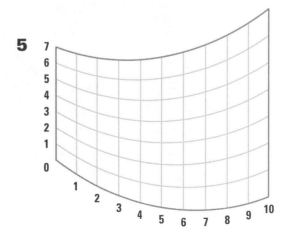

Rolling boxes

Equipment: cut-out copies of shapes

Boxes of various shapes have to be moved to a different place by rolling them end over end, not by pushing or sliding them. In each exercise, draw the symbol as it will appear each time the box is turned.

Experiment by cutting out a copy of each original shape, drawing the symbol on it and turning it as the box would roll. The first example has been started for you.

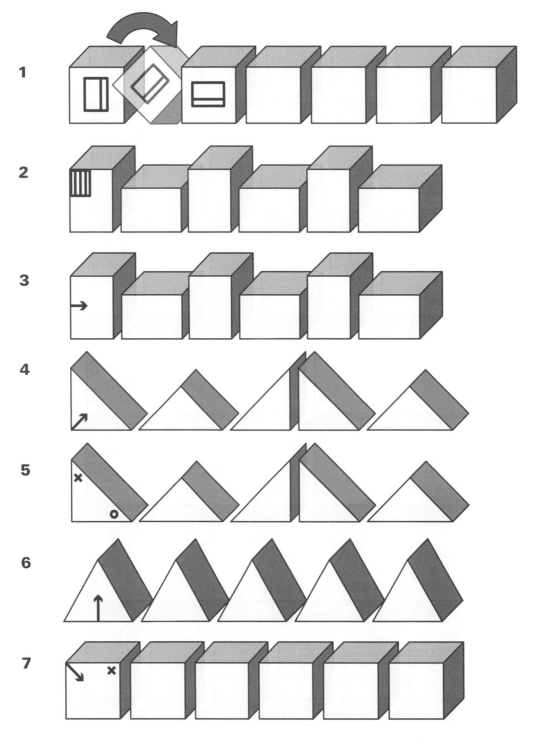

Space

Geometry and dots

This investigation can also be done using a geoboard and elastic bands.

1 Using a 3 × 3 dot paper, you can draw three different-sized squares.

How many different-sized squares can you draw using:

a a 4 × 4 dot paper?

b a 5 × 5 dot paper?

Do not forget the squares with sides at an angle or tilted, like the segments shown here.

2 Using a 3 × 3 dot paper you can draw this isosceles triangle. (An isosceles triangle has two sides equal.)

This isosceles triangle (right) is not different from the one above, as you can just turn the paper to get the same picture.

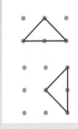

Show that there are four other different-shaped isosceles triangles that can be drawn using a 3 × 3 dot paper.

3 How many isosceles triangles can you draw within 5 × 5 dots using the marked segment as the base in each diagram?

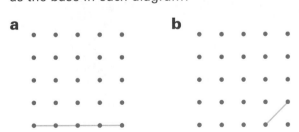

See *Teacher's Book* for diagram masters.

Challenges using cubes

Equipment: Cubes that can be joined together

1 One-centimetre yellow cubes are put together to form the six solids below.

Imagine that the outside of each solid is completely painted red and then separated again into one-centimetre cubes. For each diagram write down how many of the cubes will have exactly:

i five red faces?
ii four red faces?

a

i _____

ii _____

b

i _____

ii _____

c

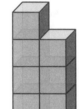

i _____

ii _____

d

i _____

ii _____

e

i _____

ii _____

f

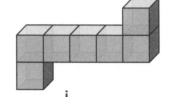

i _____

ii _____

2 Start this exercise with one little yellow one-centimetre cube. How many one-centimetre blue cubes are needed to completely cover the yellow cube and so produce a blue cube?

_____

3 Elliot used six cubes to build this staircase with three steps. How many cubes will Elliot need to make a six-step staircase?

_____

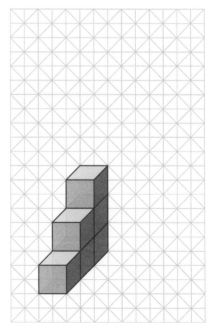

Space

74

Puzzles with shapes

Equipment: 2 cm squared paper, scissors

1 Using 2 cm squared paper, copy the five squares in this exercise (**a**–**e**) , marking in all the lines. Cut out the squares, then cut along all the lines in each one. Be sure to keep the pieces in five separate piles.

a 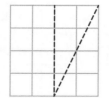   **b** 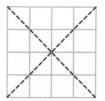   **c**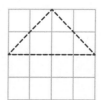

For squares **a**, **b** and **c**, take all the pieces and fit them together to make:

   i   a triangle;

   ii a rectangle;

  iii other interesting shapes.

d 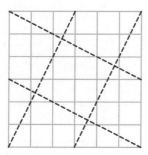   **e**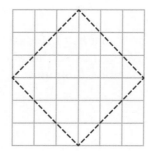

For square **d**, fit the pieces together to make five small squares all the same size.

For square **e**, fit the pieces together to make:

   i   a rectangle;

   ii a parallelogram;   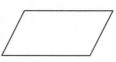

  iii a triangle.

2 Using 2 cm squared paper, copy this kite and mark in the lines. Cut out the kite, cut along all the lines, and fit the pieces together to form:

   a   a rectangle;

   b   a parallelogram.

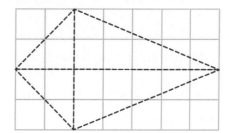

Polyominoes

Polyominoes are shapes made by joining identical (congruent) squares together, edge to edge. They were given their name in 1953 by a 22-year-old university student named Solomon Colomb.

The *monomino* is the single square:

A *domino* is made by joining two squares; there is only one domino shape:

A *triomino* is made by joining three squares: there are two triominoes:

Note: Turning (rotating) or flipping (reflecting) these shapes does not increase the number in the family of polyominoes.

These shapes are considered to be identical to the second triomino shown above.

Also note that every square must have at least one side touching a side of another, so these figures are not considered to be triominoes:

1 A *tetromino* is the shape formed by joining four squares:

Show that there are five different tetrominoes.

But remember! [ ] [ ] [ ] and [ ] [ ] [ ] are the same tetromino.

2 A *pentomino* is formed by joining five squares. There are 12 different pentomino shapes. Can you find them all and draw them?

Remember to work systematically using squared paper.

A *hexomino* is formed by joining six squares. There are 35 different hexominoes.

You may be interested to know that there are:

a 108 heptominoes (7-square polyominoes)!

b 4466 dekominoes (10-square polyominoes)!

See *Teacher's Book* for grid paper.

Tessellations

Extend each of the following tessellations for the rest of the line. Colour in your basic shapes carefully using two or four colours.

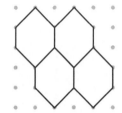

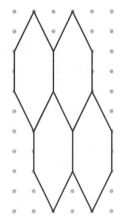

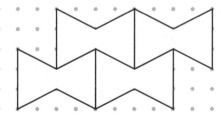

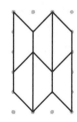

Extending tessellations

Extend each of the following tessellations for the rest of the line. Colour in your basic shapes carefully using two or four colours.

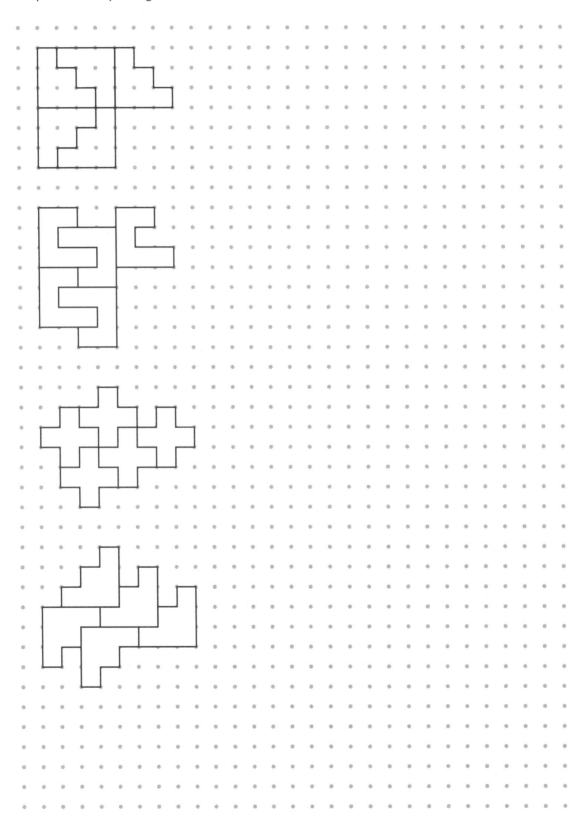

Cutting cakes

Jeffrey has a rectangular cake and needs to cut it to have equal pieces. Show how to make cuts to have the number of equal pieces needed in each question. Try to do as many questions as possible in two different ways. Study the example carefully.

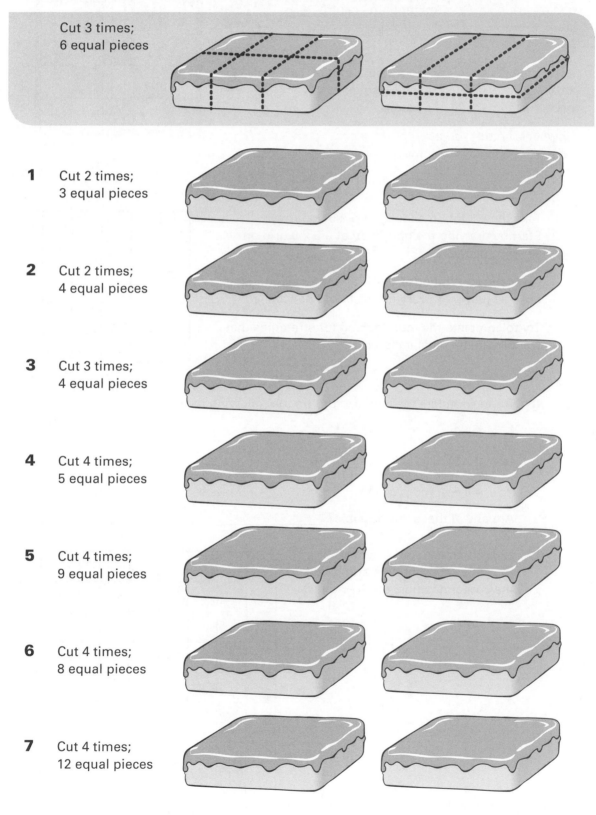

Cut 3 times;
6 equal pieces

1 Cut 2 times;
3 equal pieces

2 Cut 2 times;
4 equal pieces

3 Cut 3 times;
4 equal pieces

4 Cut 4 times;
5 equal pieces

5 Cut 4 times;
9 equal pieces

6 Cut 4 times;
8 equal pieces

7 Cut 4 times;
12 equal pieces

Knight's tour

A knight in chess moves in an L shape. Either two squares up or down and one to the right or left, or two squares to the right or left, and one up or down. So a knight in the centre could move in any of the directions shown in the diagram.

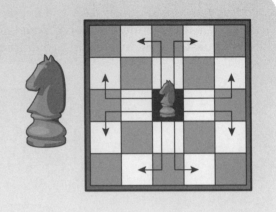

It is possible to take the knight on a tour of a chessboard, landing on every square *only once*, making a total of 64 steps.

However, before you attempt this very difficult challenge, try some simpler ones.

1 Take the knight on a tour of a 5 × 5 square. Start by drawing the boundary of a 5 × 5 grid on squared paper.

Label the starting position '1' and the position after the first jump '2'. Every jump should be labelled.

Try to complete the tour, looking for strategies that will take in the most squares.

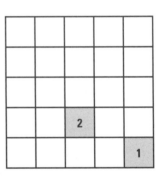

2 a Try to complete the knight's tour on the following grids:

i	6 × 6	**ii**	3 × 4
iii	4 × 3	**iv**	4 × 4
v	5 × 4	**vi**	4 × 5

Are any of these not possible? _____

b Now try to take the knight on a tour of a chessboard, starting in the corner position, on the right.

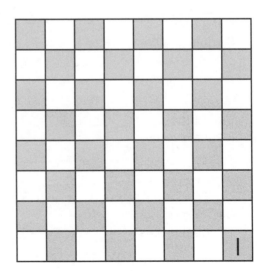

See *Teacher's Book* for grid paper.

Amazing mathematics

1 Think of a number.
Add 4.
Double the result.
Subtract 6.
Divide by 2.
Subtract the number you first thought of.

Try this with different numbers.
What do you find? _____

_____

2 Think of a number.
Multiply by 5.
Add 2.
Multiply by 2.
Subtract 4.
Divide by 10.

Try this with different numbers. What do you find? _____

_____

3 Choose any whole number.
Your number will be either even (2, 4, 6 ... 14 ... 26 ...) or
odd (1, 3, 5, 7... 13... 17...).
Step A: If it is even, divide it by 2.
Step B: If it is odd, multiply it by 3 and then add 1.
Now check your new number.
If it is even, divide it by 2.
If it is odd, multiply it by 3 and then add 1.
Again check your new number, and repeat step A or step B.
Keep going.
Will you always reach 1? _____

To take an example, start with 11.

$11 \rightarrow 11 \times 3 + 1 = 34 \rightarrow 17 \rightarrow 17 \times 3 + 1 = 52 \rightarrow 26 \rightarrow 13 \rightarrow 13 \times 3 + 1 = 40$
$\rightarrow 20 \rightarrow 10 \rightarrow 5 \rightarrow 5 \times 3 + 1 = 16 \rightarrow 8 \rightarrow 4 \rightarrow 2 \rightarrow 1.$

a What happens if you start with 12, 24 or 48?

b What happens if you start with 7, 14 or 28?

c What happens if you start with any number less than 25?

Before you start these problems, however, you should make a list of the numbers
that you already know will reach 1.

Logic using scales

In each of these statements, the first two sets of scales balance. How many ★s (stars) are needed to balance the third set of scales? Draw in the stars.

Example:

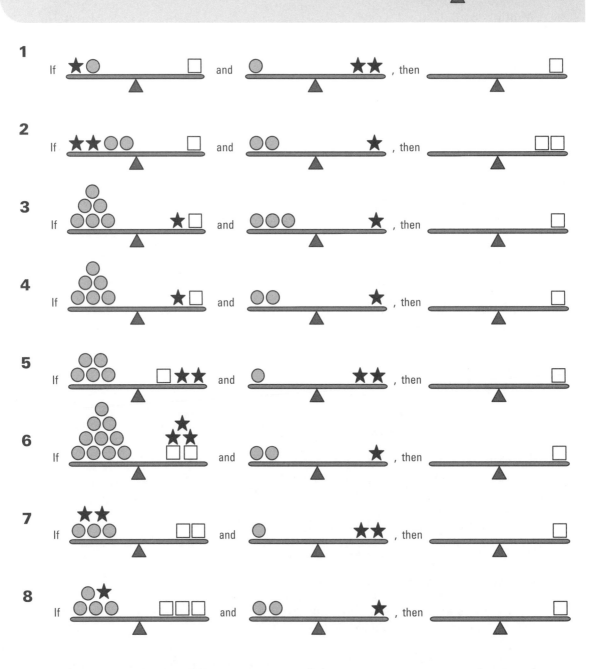

Puzzles with scales

1

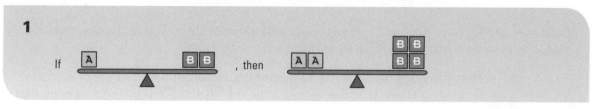

Work out how many B boxes will balance each of the scales below, using

a **A A A**

b **A A B**

c **B B / A A**

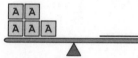

d **A A / A A A**

e **B B B / A A A**

f **A B B / A B B B**

2

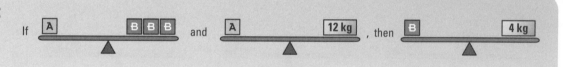

If **A ... B B B** and **A ... 12 kg** , then **B ... 4 kg**

Work out the mass of box A , if:

a **B ... 5 kg** _____

b **B 2 kg ... 8 kg** _____

c **B B ... 6 kg** _____

d **B 5 kg ... 7 kg** _____

e **A B ... 16 kg** _____

f **A A B ... 14 kg** _____

Work out the mass of box B , if:

g **A ... 12 kg** _____

h **A 1 kg ... 10 kg** _____

i **A A ... 12 kg** _____

j **A B B ... 15 kg** _____

k **A A A B ... 30 kg** _____

l **5 kg / A A B B ... 37 kg** _____

Scale puzzles

Boxes Ⓐ and Ⓑ have different masses in each of these problems. Use the first two scales to find the mass of box Ⓑ and then the mass of box Ⓐ.

First work out how many Ⓑ boxes must be placed on the left of the third set of scales. Write this on the scales. Then write the values of boxes Ⓐ and Ⓑ in the spaces provided.

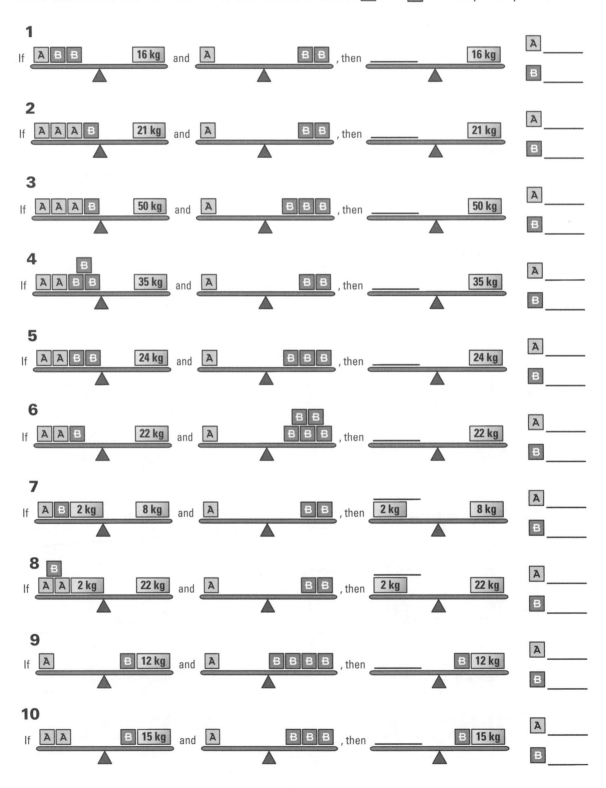

1
If Ⓐ Ⓑ Ⓑ ... 16 kg and Ⓐ ... Ⓑ Ⓑ , then _____ ... 16 kg

Ⓐ _____
Ⓑ _____

2
If Ⓐ Ⓐ Ⓐ Ⓑ ... 21 kg and Ⓐ ... Ⓑ Ⓑ , then _____ ... 21 kg

Ⓐ _____
Ⓑ _____

3
If Ⓐ Ⓐ Ⓐ Ⓑ ... 50 kg and Ⓐ ... Ⓑ Ⓑ Ⓑ , then _____ ... 50 kg

Ⓐ _____
Ⓑ _____

4
If Ⓐ Ⓐ Ⓑ Ⓑ (with Ⓑ on top) ... 35 kg and Ⓐ ... Ⓑ Ⓑ , then _____ ... 35 kg

Ⓐ _____
Ⓑ _____

5
If Ⓐ Ⓐ Ⓑ Ⓑ ... 24 kg and Ⓐ ... Ⓑ Ⓑ Ⓑ , then _____ ... 24 kg

Ⓐ _____
Ⓑ _____

6
If Ⓐ Ⓐ Ⓑ ... 22 kg and Ⓐ ... Ⓑ Ⓑ / Ⓑ Ⓑ Ⓑ , then _____ ... 22 kg

Ⓐ _____
Ⓑ _____

7
If Ⓐ Ⓑ 2 kg ... 8 kg and Ⓐ ... Ⓑ Ⓑ , then 2 kg ... 8 kg

Ⓐ _____
Ⓑ _____

8
If Ⓑ / Ⓐ Ⓐ 2 kg ... 22 kg and Ⓐ ... Ⓑ Ⓑ , then 2 kg ... 22 kg

Ⓐ _____
Ⓑ _____

9
If Ⓐ ... Ⓑ 12 kg and Ⓐ ... Ⓑ Ⓑ Ⓑ Ⓑ , then _____ ... Ⓑ 12 kg

Ⓐ _____
Ⓑ _____

10
If Ⓐ Ⓐ ... Ⓑ 15 kg and Ⓐ ... Ⓑ Ⓑ Ⓑ , then _____ ... Ⓑ 15 kg

Ⓐ _____
Ⓑ _____

Shapes and symbols

One shape or symbol is missing from each of these squares. Work out what is needed to make the patterns complete.

1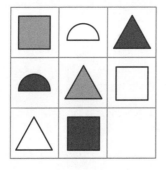

2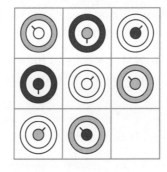

3

4

5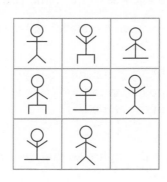

6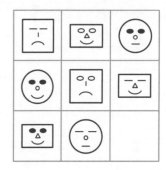

7

8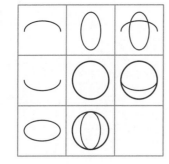

9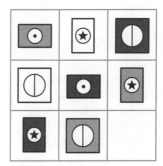

Puzzles with matches

Equipment: Use matchsticks to work out the following puzzles.

1 This shape can be built with 12 matches.

a Move 3 matches to make 3 squares all the same size.

b Move 4 matches to make 3 squares of the same size.

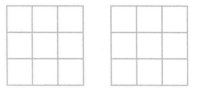

2 This shape can be built with 20 matches.

a Remove 2 matches to leave 5 squares of the same size.

b Remove 4 matches to leave 5 squares of the same size.

c Remove 4 matches to leave 4 squares.

d Move 3 matches to new positions to form 5 squares of the same size.

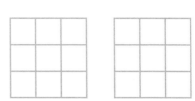

3 Remove 2 matches from this figure so that only 2 squares are left.

4 This shape can be built with 16 matches.

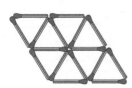

a Remove 6 matches to leave 2 triangles.

b Remove 4 matches to leave 6 triangles.

5 Use 12 matches to make 6 triangles.

6 Use 9 matches to make 5 triangles.

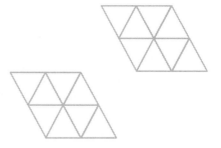

Matchstick puzzles

In each exercise, use matchsticks to build the shapes that are given above the tables.
Now continue the pattern, following the rule you have observed. Complete the table,
and use the pattern to predict the number of matches you would need for the tenth figure.

1

Number of triangles	1	2	3	4	5	→	10
Number of matches	3					→	

2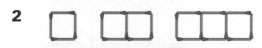

Number of squares	1	2	3	4	5	→	10
Number of matches	4					→	

3

Number of hexagons	1	2	3	4	5	→	10
Number of matches						→	

4

Number of houses	1	2	3	4	5	→	10
Number of matches						→	

5

Number of double squares	1	2	3	4	5	→	10
Number of matches						→	

6

Number of diamonds	1	2	3	4	5	→	10
Number of matches						→	

Prisoners in cells

Equipment: counters and an enlarged 3 x 3 square and 4 x 4 square

1   This diagram shows how 12 prisoners are arranged in 8 cells, with 4 prisoners in each row of 3 cells.

Now arrange 9 prisoners in the 8 cells so that there are 4 in each row of 3 cells.

How many different solutions can you find?

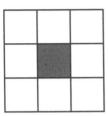 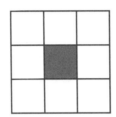 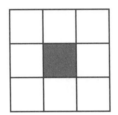 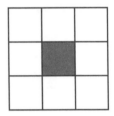

2   Place 4 prisoners in a 4 x 4 grid so that there is only one prisoner in any row or column. Here is one possible way:

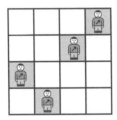

Can you find another four ways?

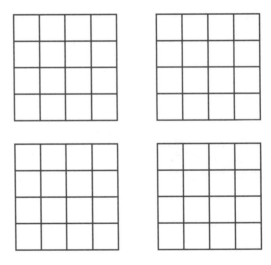

3   Place 10 prisoners in the small cells of this figure in such a way that there is an even number of prisoners in every row, in every column and in the two diagonals.

There are two different solutions.

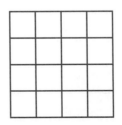 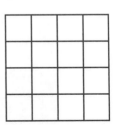

See *Teacher's Book* for these enlarged grids.

enrich-e-matics

3rd EDITION

BOOK 4

ANSWERS

Patterns and sequences (page 1)

1 21, 25, 29		**2** 51, 58, 65		**3** 24, 29, 34	
4 11, 7, 3		**5** 37, 31, 25		**6** 88, 85, 82	
7 20, 24, 28		**8** 25, 31, 37		**9** 56, 67, 78	
10 66, 77, 88		**11** 3, 3½, 4		**12** 4, 3½, 3	
13 13, 14, 17		**14** 10, 11, 13		**15** 28, 30, 37	
16 49, 47, 46		**17** 29, 25, 23		**18** 32, 25, 21	

Find my rule (page 2)

1 5, + 3	**2** 11, − 4	**3** 6, × 2	**4** 9, × 2 + 1
5 5, 10 −	**6** 13, 20 −	**7** 16, + 6	**8** 14, + 10
9 20, × 10	**10** 19, × 2 + 1	**11** 3, × 2 − 1	**12** 49, × 10 − 1
13 51, × 10 + 1	**14** 0, − 5	**15** 3, ÷ 2	
16 5, × 5	**17** 12, + 11	**18** 8, − 13	

Missing numbers (page 3)

1 12, × 6	**2** 5, − 8	**3** 28, × 4	**4** 66, × 11
5 18, × 2	**6** 17, × 2 − 1	**7** 19, × 2 + 1	**8** 59, × 10 − 1
9 14, × 10 + 4	**10** 9, ÷ 2 − 1	**11** 12, × 2 + 2	
12 15, × 3	**13** 14, × 3 − 1	**14** 25, × 3 + 1	**15** 60, × 5
16 59, × 5 − 1	**17** 5, × 3 + 2	**18** 2, × 2 − 2	**19** 1, square
20 0, square − 1			

Find two numbers (page 4)

1 4, 1	**2** 3, 2	**3** 5, 2	**4** 6, 1	**5** 3, 4
6 7, 1	**7** 5, 3	**8** 6, 2	**9** 5, 5	**10** 8, 2
11 6, 4	**12** 9, 2	**13** 6, 5	**14** 7, 4	**15** 10, 1
16 6, 6	**17** 11, 1	**18** 7, 5	**19** 8, 4	**20** 9, 3
21 6, 5	**22** 8, 3	**23** 12, 1	**24** 7, 6	**25** 10, 3
26 10, 8	**27** 11, 7	**28** 17, 1	**29** 19, 1	**30** 15, 5

Exploring numbers (page 5)

1 99	**2** 10	**3** 999	**4** 100	**5** 98
6 103	**7** 987	**8** 101	**9** 102	**10** 998
11 109	**12** 972	**13** 9	**14** 90	**15** 18
16 72	**17** 101	**18** 995	**19** 100	**20** 999

Shape values (page 6)

1 5, 4		**2** 4, 3, 5, 2, 1
3 5, 1, 3, 4, 8		**4** 2, 7, 5, 8, 1
5 4, 8, 2, 1		**6** 6, 5, 3, 1, 9
7 8, 1, 5, 7		**8** 7, 8, 2, 6, 4
9 6, 7, 4, 8		**10** 9, 4, 5, 7, 1

The four operations (page 7)

1

■		5	8	6	6	9	4	7	6	9	9	8	7	8
△		2	3	2	3	7	2	3	5	2	3	7	6	5
■ + △		7	11	8	9	16	6	10	11	11	12	15	13	13
■ − △		3	5	4	3	2	2	4	1	7	6	1	1	3
■ × △		10	24	12	18	63	8	21	30	18	27	56	42	40

2

■		4	5	7	5	3	5	4	6	7	5	5	6	8
△		3	2	2	1	2	4	2	2	1	3	2	5	7
△ × △		9	4	1	4	16	4	1	9	4	25	49		
■ + △		7	7	9	6	5	9	6	8	8	8	7	11	15
■ × △		12	10	14	5	6	20	8	12	7	15	10	30	56

3

■		4	7	2	5	8	10	7	6	8	5	9	6	10
△		3	5	1	3	1	8	2	4	2	4	4	3	3
2 × ■		8	14	4	10	16	20	14	12	16	10	18	12	20
■ − △		1	2	1	2	7	2	5	2	4	1	6	3	7
■ × △		12	35	2	15	8	80	14	24	32	20	27	18	30

4

■		9	10	12	12	24	20	24	8	36	28	18	18	21
△		3	3	6	3	5	6	4	9	4	2	6	3	
3 × △		9	6	9	18	9	15	18	12	27	12	6	18	9
■ + △		12	12	15	18	27	25	30	12	45	32	20	24	24
■ ÷ △		3	5	4	2	8	4	2	4	7	9	3	7	

Table squares (page 8)

1

+	3	5	4	8
2	5	7	6	10
7	10	12	11	15
9	12	14	13	17
6	9	11	10	14

2

+	5	3	6	4
2	7	5	8	6
7	12	10	13	11
1	6	4	7	5
8	13	11	14	12

3

+	4	1	7	8
7	11	8	14	15
12	16	13	19	20
8	12	9	15	16
1	5	2	8	9

4

+	11	5	8	6
14	25	19	22	20
10	21	15	18	16
7	18	12	15	13
3	14	8	11	9

5

+	2	9	1	8
7	9	16	8	15
5	7	14	6	13
9	11	18	10	17
3	5	12	4	11

6

+	12	3	7	9
4	16	7	11	13
8	20	11	15	17
5	17	8	12	14
7	19	10	14	16

7

+	12	14	7	3
8	20	22	15	11
1	13	15	8	4
5	17	19	12	8
7	19	14	11	10

8

+	6	10	3	8
6	12	16	9	14
5	11	15	8	13
7	13	17	10	15
10	16	20	13	18

9

+	11	5	8	12
2	13	7	10	14
5	16	10	13	17
9	19	13	16	20
6	17	11	14	18

10

+	4	5	6	9
8	12	13	14	17
2	6	7	8	11
4	8	9	10	13
7	11	12	13	16

Letters and symbols (page 9)

1 1	**2** 2	**3** 4	**4** 2	**5** 1	**6** 0
7 6	**8** 3	**9** 5	**10** 6	**11** 5	**12** 3
13 4	**14** 4	**15** 5	**16** 5		
17 2, 3 or 4, 6 or 6, 9			**18** 3, 4 or 6, 8		**19** 5, 3
20 9	**21** 3	**22** 4	**23** 7	**24** 8	**25** 4

What's my message? (page 10)

1 HAVE A GOOD WEEKEND

2 YOU ARE CLEVER

A

Square puzzles (page 11)

1 A = 3, B = 1, C = 2, D = 4, E = 5
2 A = 3, B = 5, C = 4, D = 2, E = 1
3 A = 2, B = 5, C = 1, D = 3, E = 4
4 A = 4, B = 1, C = 3, D = 2, E = 5
5 A = 4. B = 3, C = 5, D = 2, E = 1

Find the values (page 12)

1 A = 1, B = 3, C = 4, D = 2, E = 5
2 A = 3, B = 1, C = 4, D = 5, E = 2
3 A = 1, B = 2, C = 3, D = 4, E = 5
4 A = 2, B = 5, C = 4, D = 1, E = 3
5 A = 3, B = 4, C = 2, D = 5, E = 1

Odd and even (page 13)

1 a  **b** **c**

d **e** **f**

2 a **b**

These tables require students to make generalisations.

3 a even **b** even **c** even **d** even **e** even
f odd **g** even **h** odd **i** odd **j** odd
k even **l** even **m** either even or odd

Find three numbers (page 14)

1 5, 7, 4 **2** 6, 4, 8 **3** 8, 4, 11

4 8, 3, 9 **5** 2, 10, 7 **6** 12, 5, 7

7 7, 8, 9 **8** 3, 6, 12

Number sentences (page 15)

1 Some of the possible answers are listed below.

a $1 = 8 - 4 - 2 - 1$
$= 8 \div (4 \times 2 \times 1)$
$= 8 - (4 + 2) - 1$

b $2 = 8 - 4 - (2 \times 1)$
$= 8 \div 4 \div 2 + 1$
$= 8 - 4 - (2 \div 1)$

c $3 = 8 - 4 - 2 + 1$
$= 8 \div 4 + 2 - 1$
$= (8 - 4) \div 2 + 1$

d $4 = (8 \div 4) + 2 \times 1$
$= 8 \div 4 + 2 \div 1$

e $4 = (8 + 4) \div (2 + 1)$
$= (8 - 4) \div (2 - 1)$
$= (8 - 4) \times (2 - 1)$

f $5 = 8 - 4 + 2 - 1$
$= 8 \div 4 + 2 + 1$
$= 8 \div 4 \times 2 + 1$

g $6 = 8 - 4 + 2 \times 1$
$= 8 - (4 \div 2 \times 1)$
$= 8 - 4 \div 2 \times 1$

h $6 = (8 + 4) \div (2 \times 1)$
$= (8 - 4) + (2 \div 1)$
$= (8 \div 4) \times (2 + 1)$

i $7 = 8 - 4 + 2 + 1$
$= 8 - 4 \div 2 + 1$
$= (8 + 4) \div 2 + 1$

j $8 = 8 \times (4 - 2 - 1)$
$= 8 \div (4 - 2 - 1)$

k $9 = 8 + 4 - 2 - 1$
$= 8 + 4 \div 2 - 1$
$= (8 - 4) \times 2 + 1$

l $10 = 8 + 4 - 2 \times 1$
$= 8 + 4 \div 2 \times 1$
$= 8 + 4 - 2 \div 1$

m $11 = 8 + 4 \div 2 + 1$
$= 8 + 4 - 2 + 1$

n $12 = (8 + 4) \times (2 - 1)$
$= (8 + 4) \div (2 - 1)$
$= (8 - 4) \times (2 + 1)$

o $13 = 8 + 4 + 2 - 1$

p $14 = 8 + 4 + 2 \times 1$
$= 8 + 4 + 2 \div 1$

q $15 = 8 + 4 + 2 + 1$
$= 8 \times 4 \div 2 - 1$
$= 8 + 4 \times 2 - 1$

r $15 = 8 \times (4 - 2) - 1$

s $16 = 8 \times (4 \div 2) \div 1$
$= 8 \times (4 \div 2) \times 1$
$= 8 \times (4 - 2) \times 1$

t $24 = (8 + 4) \times 2 \times 1$

2 a $5 = 2 + 2 + 2 \div 2$
$5 = 2 \times 2 + 2 \div 2$
$5 = 2^2 + 2 \div 2$

b $16 = 2 \times 2 \times 2 \times 2$

c $8 = 2 \times 2 + 2 \times 2$
$8 = 2 + 2 + 2 + 2$
$8 = 2 \times 2 + 2 + 2$

d $44 = 22 + 22$

e $26 = 22 + 2 + 2$

Magic squares (page 16)

1 a

1	15	14	4
12	6	7	9
8	10	11	5
13	3	2	16

b

13	8	12	1
3	10	6	15
2	11	7	14
16	5	9	4

2 a

10	7	4	19
5	18	11	6
17	2	9	12
8	13	16	3

Magic number = 40

b

1	14	7	12
15	4	9	6
10	5	16	3
8	11	2	13

Magic number = 34

c

2	15	8	13
16	5	10	7
11	6	17	4
9	12	3	14

Magic number = 38

Square differences (page 17)

1 $5^2 - 3^2 = 2 \times 8 = 16$
$6^2 - 4^2 = 2 \times 10 = 20$

2 $6^2 - 3^2 = 3 \times 9 = 27$
$7^2 - 4^2 = 3 \times 11 = 33$

3 $7^2 - 3^2 = 4 \times 10 = 40$
$8^2 - 4^2 = 4 \times 12 = 48$

4 $8^2 - 3^2 = 5 \times 11 = 55$
$9^2 - 4^2 = 5 \times 13 = 65$

5 $9^2 - 7^2 = 2 \times 16 = 4 \times 8 = 32$
$11^2 - 9^2 = 2 \times 20 = 4 \times 10 = 40$

6 $8^2 - 6^2 = 2 \times 14 = 4 \times 7 = 28$
$10^2 - 8^2 = 2 \times 18 = 4 \times 9 = 36$

7 $4^2 - 3^2 = 4 + 3 = 7$
$5^2 - 4^2 = 5 + 4 = 9$

8 $5^2 - 1^2 = 4 \times 6 = 24$
$6^2 - 1^2 = 5 \times 7 = 35$

9 $6^2 - 2^2 = 4 \times 8 = 32$
$7^2 - 2^2 = 5 \times 9 = 45$

10 $7^2 - 6^2 + 5^2 - 4^2 = 7 + 6 + 5 + 4$
$8^2 - 7^2 + 6^2 - 5^2 = 8 + 7 + 6 + 5$

Primes (page 18)

1 a

Number	Factors	No. of factors
8	1, 2, 4, 8	4
9	1, 3, 9	3
10	1, 2, 5, 10	4
11	1, 11	2
12	1, 2, 3, 4, 6, 12	6
13	1, 13	2
14	1, 2, 7, 14	4
15	1, 3, 5, 15	4
16	1, 2, 4, 8, 16	5
17	1, 17	2
18	1, 2, 3, 6, 9, 18	6
19	1, 19	2
20	1, 2, 4, 5, 10, 20	6
21	1, 3, 7, 21	4
22	1, 2, 11, 22	4
23	1, 23	2
24	1, 2, 3, 4, 6, 8, 12, 24	8
25	1, 5, 25	3

Number	Factors	No. of factors
26	1, 2, 13, 26	4
27	1, 3, 9, 27	4
28	1, 2, 4, 7, 14, 28	6
29	1, 29	2
30	1, 2, 3, 5, 6, 10, 15, 30	8
31	1, 31	2
32	1, 2, 4, 8, 16, 32	6
33	1, 3, 11, 33	4
34	1, 2, 17, 34	4
35	1, 5, 7, 35	4
36	1, 2, 3, 4, 6, 9, 12, 18, 36	9
37	1, 37	2
38	1, 2, 19, 38	4
39	1, 3, 13, 39	4
40	1, 2, 4, 5, 8, 10, 20, 40	8

b The prime numbers have exactly two factors

c Only the squares of the prime numbers 4, 9, 25, 49, … have three factors only.

2 2, 3, 5, 7, 11, 13, 17, 19, 23, 29, 31, 37, 41, 43, 47, 53, 59, 61, 67, 71, 73, 79, 83, 89, 97.

Prime patterns (page 19)

1 a 2, 3, 5, 7, 11, 13, 17, 19, 23, 29, 31, 37, 41, 43, 47, 53, 59, 61, 67, 71, 73, 79, 83, 89, 97.

b i F **ii** A **iii** A and E **iv** 6

2 c When the numbers are in four columns, all the primes except 2 occur in columns 1 and 3.

d When the numbers are in five columns, all primes: ending in 1 are in column 1; ending in 7 are in column 2; ending in 3 are in column 3; ending in 9 are in column 4.

5 is the only prime number in column 5.

3 The square numbers shaded are all along one main diagonal and on a line next to the diagonal.

Goldbach's conjecture (page 20)

Although all possible solutions are listed here, students are not expected to find every solution.

1 6 = 3 + 3

2 8 = 3 + 5

3 12 = 5 + 7

4 14 = 7 + 7
  = 3 + 11

5 16 = 5 + 11
  = 3 + 13

6 18 = 7 + 11
  = 5 + 13

7 20 = 7 + 13
  = 3 + 17

8 22 = 11 + 11
  = 5 + 17
  = 3 + 19

9 24 = 11 + 13
  = 7 + 17
  = 5 + 19

10 26 = 13 + 13
  = 7 + 19
  = 3 + 23

11 28 = 11 + 17
  = 5 + 23

12 30 = 13 + 17
  = 11 + 19
  = 7 + 23

13 32 = 13 + 19
  = 3 + 29

14 34 = 17 + 17
  = 11 + 23
  = 5 + 29
  = 3 + 31

15 36 = 17 + 19
  = 13 + 23
  = 7 + 29
  = 5 + 31

16 38 = 19 + 19
  = 7 + 31

17 40 = 17 + 23
  = 11 + 29
  = 3 + 37

18 44 = 13 + 31
  = 7 + 37
  = 3 + 41

19 62 = 31 + 31
  = 19 + 43
  = 3 + 59

20 100 = 47 + 53
  = 41 + 59
  = 29 + 71
  = 17 + 83
  = 11 + 89
  = 3 + 97

Which number remains? (page 21)

1 8 **2** 16 **3** 15 **4** 6 **5** 4 **6** 15

7 6 **8** 16 **9** 45 **10** 9 **11** 12 **12** 25

Arrange the numbers (page 22)

Answers arranged clockwise from the top circle.

1 6 in centre, 5, 4, 3, 2, 1, 7, 8, 9, 10, 11. Line total: 18

11 in centre, 1, 2, 3, 4, 5, 10, 9, 8, 7, 6. Line total: 22

1 in centre, 2, 3, 4, 5, 6, 11, 10, 9, 8, 7. Line total: 14

Note: There are many other possible answers.

2 $\boxed{7} - \boxed{4} = \boxed{3} \times \boxed{2} = \boxed{6} - \boxed{5} = \boxed{1} + \boxed{8} = \boxed{9}$

3 a 1, 14, 12, 10 **b** 1, 4, 3, 2, 5 **c** 6, 4, 3, 2, 5

4 +91/20 +21/90 +81/30 +31/80 +71/40 +41/70 +51/60 +61/50

Remember that in these solutions you are carrying:

+95/16 +15/96 +85/26 +25/86 +75/36 +35/76 +72/39 +32/79 +62/49

+42/69 +93/18 +13/89 +63/48 +43/68 +94/17 +14/97 +84/27 +24/87

Triangle patterns (page 23)

1 4, 2, 3 **2** 1, 3, 5 **3** 4, 5, 1 **4** 9, 1, 2

5 6, 4, 5 **6** 9, 1, 5 **7** 7, 8, 3 **8** 9, 3, 5

9 3, 4, 11 **10** 1, 8, 12 **11** 2, 3, 18 **12** 3, 10, 17

What's my question? (page 24)

All the possible solutions are listed.

1 50 ×2 = 100; 25 ×4 = 100; 20 ×5 = 100

2 12 ×3 = 36; 18 ×2 = 36

3 32 ×2 = 64; 16 ×4 = 64

4 27 ×2 = 54; 18 ×3 = 54

5 24 ×2 = 48; 12 ×4 = 48; 16 ×3 = 48

6 12 ×7 = 84; 21 ×4 = 84; 28 ×3 = 84; 14 ×6 = 84

7 36 ×2 = 72; 18 ×4 = 72; 24 ×3 = 72; 12 ×6 = 72

8 48 ×2 = 96; 24 ×4 = 96; 12 ×8 = 96; 32 ×3 = 96; 16 ×6 = 96

Dartboard problems (page 25)

1 a 3, 5, 6, 8, 9, 10, 11, 12 and all further numbers are possible

b 1, 2, 4 and 7 are the only impossible scores

2 a 2, 4, 6, 7, 8, 9 and all further numbers are possible

b 1, 3, and 5 are the only impossible scores

3 22, 18 , 24 or 16.

4 a 6 **b** 17 **c** 9 + 9 = 18
6 + 6 + 6 = 18
6 + 6 + 2 + 2 + 2 = 18
6 + 2 + 2 + 2 + 2 + 2 + 2 = 18
2 + 2 + 2 + 2 + 2 + 2 + 2 + 2 + 2 = 18

Missing digits (page 26)

1 43 + 32 = 75

2 134 + 255 = 389

3 482 + 265 = 747

4 381 + 595 = 976

5 274 + 389 = 663

6 732 + 378 = 1110

7 78 − 24 = 54

8 379 − 227 = 152

9 87 − 34 = 53

10 42 − 38 = 4

11 324 − 286 = 38

12 432 − 179 = 253

13 13 × 5 = 65

14 69 × 3 = 207

15 54 × 7 = 378

16 223 × 4 = 892; 248 × 4 = 992

17 273 × 4 = 1092; 298 × 4 = 1192

18 246 × 3 = 738

19 365 × 7 = 2555

20 177 × 9 = 1593

Open-ended questions (page 27)

1 a 6, 12, 18, 24, ... any multiple of 6

b 10, 20, 30, 40, ... any multiple of 10

c 2, 3, 5, 7, 11, 13, 17, 19, 23, 29 these are all prime numbers less than 30 with exactly two factors

d 4, 9, 169 these are the squares of prime numbers and have exactly three factors

2 a 6 or 12 or 18, or any multiple of 6

b 12 or 24 or 36, or any multiple of 12

c 12 or 24 or 36, or any multiple of 12

d 10 or 20 or 30, or any multiple of 10

3 19, 28, 37 any of these numbers

4 $1 \times 2 \times 12$, $1 \times 3 \times 8$, $1 \times 4 \times 6$, $2 \times 2 \times 6$, $3 \times 2 \times 4$

5 4, 16, 36, 64

6 11, 31, 41, 61, 71

7 There are an infinite number of answers to these questions. Some possible answers are:

a $\frac{1}{2} + \frac{1}{2}$, $\frac{1}{3} + \frac{2}{3}$, $\frac{1}{4} + \frac{3}{4}$, $\frac{1}{5} + \frac{4}{5}$, $\frac{2}{5} + \frac{3}{5}$, ...

b $2 + \frac{1}{2}$, $2\frac{1}{4} + \frac{1}{4}$, $2\frac{1}{6} + \frac{2}{6}$, $1\frac{1}{4} + 1\frac{1}{4}$, ...

c $1 - \frac{1}{4}$, $2 - 1\frac{1}{4}$, $3 - 2\frac{1}{4}$, $1\frac{1}{2} - \frac{3}{4}$, $\frac{7}{8} - \frac{1}{8}$, ...

d $\frac{1}{2} \times \frac{2}{1}$, $\frac{1}{3} \times \frac{3}{1}$, $\frac{1}{4} \times \frac{4}{1}$, $\frac{3}{2} \times \frac{2}{3}$, $\frac{3}{4} \times \frac{4}{3}$, ...

What fraction's shaded? (page 28)

There are many possible solutions. Here are a few of them.

1 $\frac{1}{3}$

2 $\frac{1}{4}$

3 $\frac{2}{3}$

4 $\frac{3}{4}$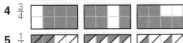

5 $\frac{1}{4}$

6 $\frac{1}{2}$

7 $\frac{1}{2}$

8 $\frac{1}{2}$  **9** $\frac{1}{2}$

10 $\frac{1}{4}$ **11** $\frac{1}{8}$ **12** $\frac{5}{8}$

Hexagon fractions (page 29)

1 $\frac{1}{6}$ **2** $\frac{1}{3}$ **3** $\frac{1}{2}$ **4** $\frac{1}{3}$ **5** $\frac{1}{3}$ **6** $\frac{1}{2}$

7 $\frac{1}{2}$ **8** $\frac{2}{3}$ **9** $\frac{1}{2}$ **10** $\frac{1}{6}$ **11** $\frac{1}{12}$ **12** $\frac{5}{12}$

Pizza maths (page 30)

1 3 **2** 3 **3** 4 **4** 2 **5** 2

6 4 **7** 6 **8** 8 **9** 9 **10** 4

Problem-solving fractions (page 31)

1 $50 **2** $150 **3** $48 **4** $60

Problems with fractions (page 32)

1 $50 **2 a** $6 **b** $36

3 a $20 **b** $80 **4 a** $120 **b** $720

Number machine (page 33)

1 a 6 **b** 6 **c** 8 or 7 **d** 14 or 13

2 a i 19 → 10 → 5 → 3 → 2 → 1

ii 28 → 14 → 7 → 4 → 2 → 1

b i 6 or 5 **ii**

Where's the number? (page 34)

1 a

L	M	N	O	P	Q	R
18		17		16		15
	19		20		21	
25		24		23		22

b Q **c** R **d** O **e** Q **f** R

2 a

T	U	V	W	X	Y	Z
28	27	26	25	24	23	22
29	30	31	32	33	34	35
42	41	40	39	38	37	36
43	44	45	46	47	48	49

b T **c** Z **d** T **e** T **f** Z

Money problems (page 35)

1 a 50 c **b** 40 c **c** 25 c

2 a $60, $40 **b** $75, $25 **c** $95, $5

3 $5, $5 **4** $35, $32

5 4, 1, $1.60 **6** 6, 3

7 a 2, 8 **b** 6, 4 **c** 2, 10 **d** 8, 4

At the market (page 36)

1 a 5 **b** 10 **c** 10 **d** 15

2 a 2 **b** 6

3 a 1 kg **b** 3 kg **c** 3 kg **d** 1·5 kg

4 a 25 **b** 30 **5** 50c

Shopping (page 37)

1 $32 **2** $4.50 **3 a** $35 **b** $63

4 80c **5 a i** 1 **ii** 10 **iii** 3

b i $1.25 **ii** $2.25 **iii** $7.50

6 a i $6 **ii** $2 **iii** 75c **iv** $1.25

b i $6 **i** $1.20 **i** $2.40 **i** 80c

7 $2

Missing shapes (page 38)

1 ◇ ■ **2** ● △ **3** □ △ **4** ○ ●

5 ▷ ▤ **6** ╲ ● **7** D D **8** M D

9 ★ ★ **10** ● ○

Halves and quarters (page 39)

1 These are only some of the possible solutions.

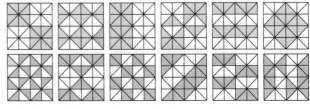

D

2

How many possibilities? (page 40)

1 a i $8 \times 1, 4 \times 2$ **ii** $12 \times 1, 4 \times 3, 6 \times 2$
  iii $14 \times 1, 7 \times 2$ **iv** $18 \times 1, 9 \times 2, 6 \times 3$
  v $21 \times 1, 7 \times 3$ **vi** $20 \times 1, 10 \times 2, 5 \times 4$
  vii $25 \times 1, 5 \times 5$ **viii** $24 \times 1, 12 \times 2, 8 \times 3, 6 \times 4$

  b 24   The rectangles are $24 \times 1, 12 \times 2, 8 \times 3, 6 \times 4$

2 a 12   15, 16, 18, 51, 56, 58, 61, 65, 68, 81, 85, 86

  b 6   16, 18, 56, 58, 68, 86   **c** 6   61, 65, 68   81, 85, 86

3 a 3 pairs   **b** 10 pairs   **c** 45 pairs

4 15 matches

Counting techniques (page 41)

1 a 6 possibilities   **b** 9 possibilities

  56 57   55 56 57
  65 67   65 66 67
  75 76   75 76 77

2 a 6 possibilities

  567 576 657 675 756 765

  b 27 possibilities

  555 556 557 565 566 567 575 576 577
  655 656 657 665 666 667 675 676 677
  755 756 757 765 766 767 775 776 777

3 List the possibilities starting with 5:

5678 5768 5867 5687 5786 5876

If we start with 6, 7 or 8, in each case there are again 6 possibilities, and so there is a total of 24.   or

List all 24 possibilities, working systematically.

4 a i 3   **ii** 11   **iii** 2
  b i 19   **ii** 19   **iii** 8

What chance? (page 42)

1 a 2 chances out of 20 or 1 chance in 10

  b Person brought a sandwich from home

2 There are many different possible ways of shading the rectangles.

  a shade any 3 out of the 15 rectangles.

  b no shading at all.   **c** shade all rectangles

  d shade any 5 out of the 20 rectangles

3 a 120   **b** 3 chances out of 12 or 1 chance in 4

  c orange   **d** 5

  e red = 10, blue = 5, yellow = 15, orange = 20, green = 10

Spinner probabilities (page 43)

1 3 chances out of 25, $\frac{3}{25}$ **2** $\frac{2}{25}$

3 6   **4** $\frac{13}{25}$ **5** 2 and 10 or 3 and 9 or 4 and 8 or 5 and 7

6 0   **7** $\frac{6}{25}$ **8** $\frac{3}{25}$

Picture graphs (page 44)

1 a $25 \times 5 = 125$ **b** bus   **c** taxi

  d 25   **e** tram

2 a 15   **b** Monday and Thursday
  c 21   **d** Tuesday   **e** $35 \times 3 = 105$

Picture this (page 45)

1 a 18   **b** 15   **c** 12   **d** chips   **e** pies, 3
  f $28 \times 3 = 84$ **g** 9 left (6 sold)

2 a i 24   **ii** 8   **iii** 6   **iv** 18

  b 72

Graphs (page 46)

1

George	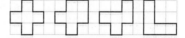					
Emanuel						
Laura	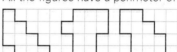					
Phoebe						
Mimi						

2 a 2 km   **b** 1 hour   **c** 3 km

  d Faster. She travelled 3 km in 1 hour to George and only 2 km in 1 hour to Helena.

3 a 12   **b** 36

Sector graph (page 47)

1 a 2 hours   **b** 4 hours

2 a 12 hours   **b** 6 hours   **c** 36 hours

3 a 5 hours   **b** 15 hours   **c** 20 hours

Perimeter (page 48)

1 4, 5, 6, 7

2 a 38 cm   **b** 42 cm   **c** 42 cm   **d** 46 cm   **e** 44 cm   **f** 70 cm

Find the perimeter (page 49)

1 a All the figures have a perimeter of 12 cm.

Some other shapes with a perimeter of 12 cm

  b All the figures have a perimeter of 16 cm.

Some other shapes with a perimeter of 16 cm

2 They will arrive at school at exactly the same time. (Diane's path is not really a shortcut.)

Area investigation (page 50)

1 a, c, d, f, g, h, i, j

2 These are only some of the possible shapes. For both **2a** and **2b** there are many other possible solutions.

  a

  b

Perimeter and area (page 51)

1

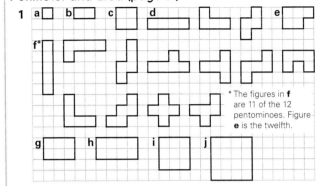

* The figures in **f** are 11 of the 12 pentominoes. Figure **e** is the twelfth.

Taping boxes (page 52)

1 a 20 + 8 + 20 + 8 = 56 cm
  b 50 cm   **c** 10 cm   **d** 5 cm
2 a Tape = 2 × length + 2 × width + 4 × height
      = 2 × 20 + 2 × 6 + 4 × 8
      = 84 cm
  b 70 cm   **c** 15 cm   **d** 7 cm

Show the temperature (page 53)

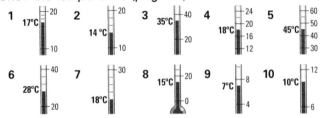

1 17°C **2** 14 °C **3** 35°C **4** 18°C **5** 45°C
6 28°C **7** 18°C **8** 15°C **9** 7°C **10** 10°C

Match the answer (page 54)

1 C	**2** E	**3** D	**4** A	**5** B
6 D	**7** C	**8** A	**9** E	**10** B
11 D	**12** E	**13** B	**14** C	**15** A
16 C	**17** E	**18** B	**19** A	**20** D

Measurement using tables (page 55)

1 a 550 g, 450 g   **b** 850g, 350g
2 $16, $8   **3** 16 kg, 8 kg, 11 kg
4 4 packages, 8, $1.20
5 **Bananas** 4, 3, 2, 1, 0, $2\frac{2}{3}$, $1\frac{1}{5}$
  Grapes 0, $\frac{3}{4}$, $1\frac{1}{2}$, $2\frac{1}{4}$, 3, 1, 2

Fractions in measurement (page 56)

1 a $3   **b** $1\frac{3}{4}$ kg
2 200 mL
3 a 200 cm   **b** 180 cm
4 a 36 L   **b** $54   **c** 528 km
5 a 160 ml   **b** 200 mL
6 a $2.50   **b** $3.75   **c** $25
7 $1\frac{1}{2}$ hours

Questioning time (page 57)

1 12 mins.   **2** 28 mins.   **3** 9 hrs 46 mins.
4 a 16 hours   **b** 7 p.m.
5 11 hours 30 minutes   **6** 41 hours 40 minutes
7 9:50 a.m.   **8** 9:15 p.m.   **9** 6:48 p.m.   **10** 12:12 p.m.

Time challenges (page 58)

1 Monday
2 a Wednesday   **b** Monday   **c** Friday
3 a 25 days   **b i** Saturday   **ii** 9 days
  c 80 months   **d** 2 years 4 months
4 Saturday   **5** 28 days later

Multiple choice—measurement (page 59)

1 A, C	**2** B, D	**3** B	**4** A	**5** D	**6** A
7 A, C	**8** A, C, D	**9** B, C	**10** A	**11** B	**12** B

Measurement problems (page 60)

1 A	**2** A	**3** B	**4** D	**5** B	**6** D
7 A, C	**8** A	**9** A	**10** D	**11** A	

Packing cans (page 61)

1 a l = 30 cm   w = 20 cm   h = 12 cm
  b l = 30 cm   w = 30 cm   h = 24 cm
2 24
3

Ways that cans are packed	length	width	height
4 × 3 × 1	40	30	12
3 × 2 × 2	30	20	24
2 × 2 × 3	20	20	36
4 × 1 × 3	40	10	36
1 × 3 × 4	10	30	48
1 × 2 × 6	10	20	72
1 × 1 × 12	10	10	144

Speed challenges (page 62)

1 a 300 m   **b** 4500 m = 4.5 km
  c 2 minutes   **d** 40 minutes
2 a 400 metres   **b** 6 km
  c 120 seconds = 2 minutes   **d** 10 minutes
3 a 225 km   **b** 30 km
  c 4 hours   **d** 1 hour 40 minutes
4 a 126 km   **b** 21 km
  c 2 hours   **d** 45 minutes

Rate problems (page 63)

1 a 30 L   **b** 400 L   **c** 370 L
2 a 4200 times   **b** 40 minutes
3 a 400 metres   **b** 40 metres
  c 15 seconds
4 a $3   **b** 30 c   **c** $90   **d** 20 hours
5 a 8 hours   **b** $2\frac{1}{2}$ hours   **c** 10 m²   **d** 2 m²

Water flow (page 64)

1 1200 litres
2 a i 100 litres   **ii** 300 litres
  b 30 seconds   **c** 150 litres   **d** 400 litres
3 a 20 litres   **b** 120 litres
4 a 180 mL   **b** 10800 mL = 10.8 L
5 1500 mL= 1.5 L

Cough medicine (page 65)

1 5 times   **2** 5 mL   **3** 25 mL   **4** 50 doses
5 10 days   **6** 150 mL   **7** Friday 2 p.m.   **8** $1.50

Travel graphs (page 66)

1 Amie   **2** Carla   **3** Ben and Amie

4 3 hours   **5** 25 km/h

6 Ben's speed = $\frac{30}{4}$ = 7.5 km/h and

Amie's speed = $\frac{70}{4}$ = 17.5 km/h. Amie's speed is greater.

7
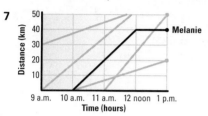

Marbles (page 67)

1 15 mL, 195 mL   **2** 8 mL, 224 mL

3 8 mL, 224 ml   **4** 20 mL, 280 mL

Fuel tank (page 68)

1 20 L, 10 L, used 10 L   **2** 40 L, 20 L, used 20 L

3 45 L, 15 L, used 30 L   **4** 24 L, 8 L, used 16 L

5 24 L, 12 L, used 12 L   **6** 28 L, 14 L, used 14 L

7 36 L, 9 L, used 27 L   **8** 24 L, 6 L, used 18 L

Mass (page 69)

1 1430 g = 1.43 kg   **2** 2125 g = 2.125 g   **3** 24

4 140 kg   **5** 20   **6** 20   **7** 48   **8** 10

9 3.2 kg   **10** 6   **11 a** 32 kg **b** 40 kg   **12** 43 kg

13 a $8   **b** $12   **c** $24   **d** $20

How many? (page 70)

1 a 7, 2, 9   **b** 4, 1, 1, 6   **c** 9, 4, 1, 14   **d** 7, 6, 2, 2, 17

2 a 4, 1, 5   **b** 9, 3, 1, 13   **c** 10, 4, 14   **d** 18, 8, 2, 28

Amazing graphs (page 71)

Rolling boxes (page 72)

7

Geometry and dots (page 73)

1 a 5 squares

   b 8 squares

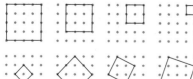

(page 73 continued)

2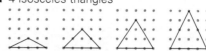

3 a 4 isosceles triangles

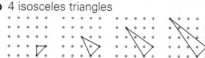

   b 4 isosceles triangles

Challenges using cubes (page 74)

1 a i 2 **ii** 1   **b i** 1 **ii** 3   **c i** 1 **ii** 3

   d i 2 **ii** 4   **e i** 0 **ii** 4   **f i** 2 **ii** 5

2 26 blue cubes

3 15 more cubes: 4 + 5 + 6. Altogether 21 cubes

Puzzle with shapes (page 75)

1 a i   **ii**   **iii**

   b i   **ii**   **iii**
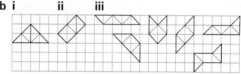

   c i   **ii**   **iii**

   d   **e i**

   ii   **iii**
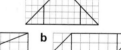

2 a   **b**

Polyominoes (page 76)

1 These are the four tetrominoes.

2 The pentominoes can be identified by letters.

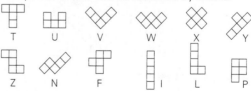

T   U   V   W   X   Y

Z   N   F   I   L   P

Tessellations (page 77)

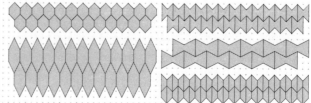

Extending tessellations (page 78)

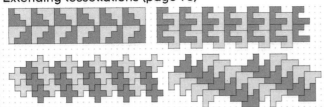

Cutting cakes (page 79)

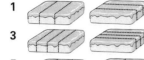

Knight's tour (page 80)

Possible solutions are given for each one, all of which are the work of students. There are many other solutions.

1 5 × 5 square

5	20	11	16	25
12	17	6	21	10
7	4	19	24	15
18	13	2	9	22
3	8	23	14	1

2 a i 6 × 6 square

19	28	15	6	21	30
14	5	20	29	16	7
27	18	35	8	31	22
4	13	26	17	36	9
25	34	11	2	23	32
12	3	24	33	10	1

ii 3 × 4 grid

8	11	6	3
5	2	9	12
10	7	4	1

iii 4 × 3 grid

12	5	10
9	2	7
6	11	4
3	8	1

iv There is no solution to the 4 × 4 square.

v 5 × 4 grid

18	13	4	9
3	8	19	14
12	17	10	5
7	2	15	20
16	11	6	1

vi 4 × 5 grid

12	9	18	5	14
17	4	13	10	19
8	11	2	15	6
3	16	7	20	1

b 8 × 8 square

7	18	35	46	9	20	37	48
34	45	8	19	36	47	10	21
17	6	55	58	63	60	49	38
44	33	64	61	54	57	22	11
5	16	43	56	59	62	39	50
30	27	32	53	42	25	12	23
15	4	29	26	13	2	51	40
28	31	14	3	52	41	24	1

Amazing mathematics (page 81)

1 Result is always 1

2 Result is number you first thought of

3 Note that from the example, any starting number from the chain (11 → 34 → 17 → 52 → 26 → 13 → 40 → 20 → 10 → 5 → 16 → 8 → 4 → 2 → 1) will reach 1.

In fact, any even multiple from the chain will also reach 1.

a 12 reaches 1, and hence so do 24 and 48

b 7 reaches 1, and hence so do 14, and 28.

c We already know the following numbers reach 1, as they occur in the chains above: 2, 3, 4, 5, 6, 7, 8, _, 10, 11, 12, _, 14, _ 16, _, _, _, 20, _, 22, _, 24
The missing numbers will all reach 1.

Logic using scales (page 82)

1 3　　**2** 6　　**3** 1　　**4** 2　　**5** 8　　**6** 1　　**7** 4　　**8** 1

Puzzles with scales (page 83)

1 a 6　　**b** 5　　**c** 6　　**d** 10　　**e** 9　　**f** 9

2 a 15 kg　**b** 18 kg　**c** 9 kg　**d** 6 kg　**e** 12 kg　**f** 6 kg

　　g 4 kg　**h** 3 kg　**i** 2 kg　**j** 3 kg　**k** 3 kg　**l** 4 kg

Scale puzzles (page 84)

1 A = 8 kg　**2** A = 6 kg　**3** A = 15 kg　**4** A = 10 kg
　　B = 4 kg　　　B = 3 kg　　　B = 5 kg　　　B = 5 kg

5 A = 9 kg　**6** A = 10 kg　**7** A = 4 kg　**8** A = 8 kg
　　B = 3 kg　　　B = 2 kg　　　B = 2 kg　　　B = 4 kg

9 A = 16 kg　**10** A = 9 kg
　　B = 4 kg　　　B = 3 kg

Shapes and symbols (page 85)

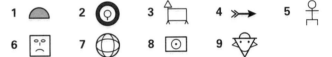

Puzzles with matches (page 86)

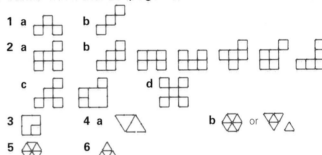

Matchstick puzzles (page 87)

1 5, 7, 9, 11, → 21　　2 × □ + 1

2 7, 10, 13, 16, → 31　　3 × □ + 1

3 6, 11, 16, 21, 26, → 51　　5 × □ + 1

4 5, 9, 13, 17, 21, → 41　　4 × □ + 1

5 7, 12, 17, 22, 27, → 52　　5 × □ + 2

6 4, 9, 14, 19, 24, → 49　　5 × □ − 1

Prisoners in cells (page 88)

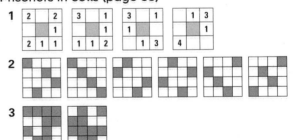

H